A
Chronology
of
Librarianship

by

Josephine Metcalfe Smith

The Scarecrow Press, Inc.
Metuchen, N. J.   1968

Affectionately dedicated to my son,
because he said:
Mother, I am so proud of you

A Preface to the Tables

This chronology presents the historical data
found in library literature, including some that are du-
bious and many that need to be verified by further research.

While it covers data from the beginning of the
Christian era, this chronology emphasizes librarianship
in the United States, and it is more concerned with
service than with persons or historic collections. It
attempts a beginning toward fulfilling what our British
colleague, Richard Garnett, asked for: a "bringing together what must now be laboriously hunted up."

This work does not propose to establish dates,
only to report them as found. Following the initial entry for each item there will be given, in parentheses,
a citation; this is the source of the date under which an
occurrence is entered. If further information from that
source is included in the item, a semicolon follows the
curves. Unless accompanying facts are a part of common knowledge, reference is made to other sources used.

To make citing as unobtrusive and useful as possible, an abbreviated form was devised. It is coded to
the Bibliography found at the end of the Tables. For
example, (Downs p. 33) refers to Downs, Robert B.,
Union Catalogs in the United States, while (*Downs p.
2) refers to Downs, Robert B., The First Freedom.
The Bibliography is arranged alphabetically by the code
symbol assigned to each work, with abbreviations standing first in their respective categories. Examples of
the latter are (AmLA 1959, p. 180) refering to The
Bowker Annual, 1959 edition; (EB ed. 11, v. 16, p.
550) refering to the Encyclopaedia Britannica, eleventh
edition, volume 16.

The original plan was to enter in the Tables only
those occurrences for which there is an exact date and
a citation. But this would have caused the omission of
a great amount of interesting and useful material.

Every effort has been made to follow the rule about citations, but in the interest of historiographic curiosity the rule about exact date has been strained in a few instances, e. g. at 700; 1400; 1930. In other instances an occurrence without exact date has been added to a related event for which a date has been established. This is done in an attempt to show trends, interests and problems in our field.

Setting the internal dates from the first century of the Christian era to 1960 is intended to show the chain of events which has led to today's library services. The beginning is at the first century because a number of evolutions which occurred in that era appear essential to our concept of acceptable service. The terminus has been set at 1959 because the major trends (in the library field) of this century seem to have been set by this date; occurrences of the 1960's are still developmental. But here again the purely historiographic interests would be left out. For that reason, the user will find some information concerning events outside the date limits set above.

To extend the usefulness of the Tables, two indexes have been prepared. The Subject Index proposes to pull together, under broad headings, the varied facts presented in the Tables, suggesting the many aspects of librarianship. For example, a concise history of the book, per se, can be traced under Book: Form & Make-Up; under Professional Journals, one can find a representative listing beginning at 1876; under Propaganda Agent, one can find how the library has been so used. Aspects of the Public Library Movement, of Education (for librarianship), of Reference Service are listed under these headings. If the user asks what has the library done about the handicapped, he will find under the heading Service-to-the-Handicapped sub-entries for the Blind, including Braille writing and the Talking-book; for the Deaf; the Hospital patient; the Shut-in; and for Bibliotherapy. The Subject Index is for the user seeking an overview in some area of librarianship.

If the user is searching for a specific fact or occurrence, he should use the Name Index, e. g., a title (Library Journal); a person (Thomas James); a place (Bobbio Monastery); a thing (Blaeu Press). Both indexes are cross-referenced, and further cross-referencing is made within the Tables to bring related matter to the attention of the user. The indexes supplement the Chronological Tables. They cite the date of entries rather than the page number.

The user will probably find the 1900's the most unsatisfactory era; its events are "too much with us." While past events are elusive, current events have not solidified. Since the library field is related to social trends, the chronology reports experiments, surveys, studies and reports, pilot projects and the like, e. g., in civil service, labor unions, certification and automation. Some events included in each century are there because they represent our cultural background (the "civilization" of librarianship, if one prefers). Events in the Dark Ages attempt only to show how we had clung to a thin thread of literacy and preservation. The possibility for library service to the general public received its first impetus from the invention of the printing press. Every step from there was progressive, but nearly every step had a precedent in the centuries before 1454. This chronology does not attempt to hide our failures; our mistakes have been duly recorded along with our accomplishments.

This work's sole raison d'etre is "to present in one source" and "to see in context" what has been happening in the field of librarianship.

Acknowledgement is hereby made of the aid and encouragement received from a host of persons, too great a number to name individually. Especial gratitude is expressed to the following, who each in his own way contributed to bringing this work to press: William B. Todd, bibliographer, Hartsell Young, associate librarian, University of Texas; James Newcomer, Texas Christian University; Thomas M. Bogie, Dallas Public Library; and Dorothy M. Crosland, director of libraries, Georgia Institute of Technology. Very special thanks are due Robert L. Collison, BBC librarian, without whom the indices would never have been done.

Table of Contents

Introduction

It is the lack of understanding and knowledge
of the history of their disciplines which make
so many American scholars lacking in matu-
rity of judgement. Efficiency is no substitute for understanding. --Randolph Adams[1]

In the library . . . eternal vigilance is
needed. --Carl Weber[2]

Randolph Adams strikes us at our weakest point.
Let us not flinch from it, but, applying Carl Weber's
dictum, let us meet the challenge; without destroying
efficiency, let us mature our judgement.
  But how shall we learn without a history? Library
Service, as a discipline, is influenced by many disciplines. Although we may not be able to decide whether
our profession is an economy, a -ship, a service, or a
science, we are agreed that it is a separate discipline.
It follows, therefore, that we have a separate history.
We should no longer be content with checklists of historical collections and bibliographical institutions, and
directories of outstanding librarians; we should lay hold
on the whole field of our discipline and seek to describe
it in full. Kohl is quoted in the Smithsonian Report for
1856 as saying:

No one can justly appreciate the value of existing information who does not know by what
exertions it has been acquired. No man can
rightly estimate any truth who is not aware
of the previous errors through which the way
to it has led. [3]

Let us, therefore, demand our full legacy, review the
past, face our errors squarely, go on to greater
achievements. And let us begin by charting our way

11

by means of a chronology.

"Without a trustworthy chronology, history would be a darksome chaos," quotes Helen R. Keller, from Francois Clément, on the motto page of her Dictionary of Dates (Macmillan, 1934). David Talboys, a staunch defender of chronology, says in the preface to his Annales Antiquitates (Oxford, 1838), "It is an auxiliary . . . without whose aid . . . the eye of History is quenched." Alfred Mayer, in the preface to his Annals of European Civilization (Cassell, 1949) sums it all up in less flowery language, "I am abundantly convinced that chronology is a necessary . . . aid to historical research." The framework of our history, then, should be a strong chronology. And the chronology can be strong, even at those points where authorities most disagree, by letting it play the devil's advocate, spark a controversy, draw out disputants and potential scientific researchers.

As keepers of the stored knowledge, we rank with theology, medicine and law as one of the oldest professions. If we are willing to go along with Richardson, we can trace our history back to creation: ". . . by many all creation was looked on as a library. . . . The whole firmament was thus a library of celestial tablets."[4] This idea makes the whole world become a storehouse of knowledge for man to retrieve. Today's "books" of sounds and punches may not be any more strange than leaves of trees or celestial tablets. The very first retriever, i.e., librarian, may have been the Devil or may have been woman, but "man" was the patron and paid for getting an erroneous "drop" from his retrieval system.

Richardson traces the library, as a storehouse and dispenser of knowledge, through each period of recorded history. He describes the imaginary libraries of the antedeluvian period: the preadamite and Adamite; the subhuman, e.g., memory libraries of animals, and the annual records of growth of a tree; the precosmic libraries of the gods, e.g., the classified circulating library of Brahma, and the mead, or knowledge, kept in jars. Among the prehistoric ones he lists the memory, the mnemonic and the picture libraries. Then Richardson moves into the period of historic libraries,

using the invention of phonetic writing as the beginning
of this period. Here he lists them as: a) temple, b)
royal archive, c) private, d) public.[5]

Thompson tells us that the first libraries of historic times were in the temples of ancient Egypt, and
that there were royal libraries in Phonecia as early as
the beginning of the eleventh century B.C.[6] The most
famous royal library was that of Assurbanipal at Nine-
veh. The first of the great private libraries may have
been as early as Pisistratus of Athens, and Polycra-
tes, tyrant of Samas.[7] It is possible that private libraries began in the fourth century B.C. with Euripi-
des, and include those of Plato and Aristotle.[8]

The origin of public libraries, as opposed to private libraries, is more difficult to establish. There
are two strong claims. One, that of Aulus Gellius, holds
that the tyrant Pisistratus established the first public
library at Athens as early as 500 years before the
Christian era. The other asserts that the public library first appeared in Rome during the last years
of the pre-Christian era, when Asinius Pollio fulfilled
Caesar's dream. The modern research library has its
prototype in "the incomparable resources of the first real
and greatest collection of intellectual materials or data
ever assembled in antiquity: the Library of Alexandria."[9] Whether you take Richardson with a pinch of
salt or a pinch of snuff, libraries, as storehouses of
knowledge, have existed in some form for a long, long
time, and Keepers, by whatever name, have always
been necessary.

What is this "whole field" of our discipline? It
should be taken to mean an acquaintance with and ap-
preciation for: book and non-book forms; book production (ink, paper, binding); printing; publishing and presses; bibliographic description and control, research, retrieval; censorship; copyright; graphic arts; cooperative
ventures and associations; mechanical processes and
devices; the physical plant; the stock-in-trade and the
stocking of the library; the personnel, its training and
administration; legislation; education; the library's public and the library in society. These have auxiliary
aspects which claim our attention also, e.g., photography; data processing; translation, indexing, and ab-

13

stracting services; aids for the handicapped; the government as a publisher, and many others.

A library does not need a "book" to be a library. Taking Richardson's definition that a book is "any record of thought in words . . . and define a word as 'any sign for any thing,' and again explain the sign as anything which points to something other than itself,"[10] then the tree's rings of growth and Assurbanipal's clay tablets and the Christian codices are all equally books. Similarly, the microfiche, the punched card, the computer memory, and even the lowly pamphlet, may be called a book. But usually librarians prefer to think of the book as a distinct physical entity with its origin somewhere in the first century of the Christian era. We agree with L. Quincy Mumford, who, in a recent address, pointed out that in man's search for adequate means to record his thoughts, the book has proved to be one of the most adaptable and simple machines invented for conveying knowledge:

> It is portable, easily stored, simple to use,
> inexpensive, and relatively permanent. A
> book can be used by people of widely varying
> skills and levels of intelligence; it can be op-
> erated at variable speeds; it requires little
> maintenance.[11]

A study of its format and production is essential to an understanding of the extent of growth and the rate of growth of our services.

The codex form came into being without paper or printing or a press ink or a binding and casing process, but the development of all these made the book the desirable "conveyer of knowledge" it has become. Carter says, "Of all the world's inventors these two [Ts'ai Lun and Gutenberg] stand out pre-eminent in the cause of literature and education."[12] Clapperton goes even further, "The papermaker must come first to give the printer something to work on; and he should also come before the author, as the latter must have something to scribble on!"[13] It is difficult in mid-twentieth century, when in one calendar year the average consumption of paper per person can be in the hundreds of pounds, of

which almost as much is used for wrapping paper as
for printed matter, to fully appreciate the marvel of
paper. The double quatrain of Thomas Churchyard,
written in 1588, still expresses the importance of this
utilitarian invention:

> I prayse the man, that first did Paper make,
> the only thing that sets all virtues forth:
> It shoes new bookes, and keeps old workes
> awake,
> much more of price than all this world is
> worth;
> Though partchment duer, a greater time and
> space,
> yet can it not, put paper out of place:
> For paper still from man to man doth go,
> when partchment comes in few mans hands,
> you knowe. [14]

Neither can we, with five hundred years of use behind
us, fully comprehend the marvel of printing. Hunter
says that "the progress of man . . . may be divided
into three . . . evolutions . . . . Speaking . . . . Draw-
ing . . . . Printing. "[15] The quality and quantity of today's library service does not seem possible without
press printing to reduce costs, speed production, mul-
tiply copies.
   Paper making was brought into Europe in the
twelfth century, and a forerunner to press-ink was mix-
ed at that time; in the mid-fifteenth century, press
printing was brought to perfection. After that the success of the book as a cheap purveyor of knowledge was
assured. This history is part of our discipline, as is
the origin of roman script in the first century A.D.,
the development of the arabic numeral system in the
twelfth century, the continuing experiments with printing, including type cutting, plates, developments of
mechanical presses and papermaking machines, the
testing of binding materials and methods.
   We may also claim, as part of our heritage, the
history of the "internal format" of the book, including
its use of catchwords and signatures and tables of contents and errata notices and the evolution of the title

page. A. W. Pollard is quoted as saying, "It is hard to understand how the first printers who had introduced so mighty a revolution . . . hesitated for so long over so simple and so sorely needed a reform as . . . the title page."[16] There is a romantic and adventuresome history in this wedding of incipit and explicit, this coming together of "here beginneth" and "finishing stroke," this successor to the colophon, this first cousin to the titulus--and it belongs to us.

Although the book takes first place in our affections, we are pleased to make use of and note the history of the production of all non-book forms, e.g., maps, music, graphic and plastic art, discs, tapes, photographic media, periodicals (journals, newspapers, etc.), computer tapes and memories, and even the much maligned group that includes the pamphlet, the brochure, the leaflet, the broadside. Any form from which recorded knowledge can be retrieved is of interest to the librarian.

The annals of book selection are a part of our history. A "Recommended Reading List" has been reported as early as 1494, and 1793 saw the first catalog of selected books to appear in this country.

After "book selection" must come bibliographic description. "What do you read, my lord?" asks Polonius; "Words, words, words," answers Hamlet. But fortunately that is not always true and librarians are not mere dispensers of words. Whether he is aware of it or not, every patron wants a particular book and the library cannot afford to be unaware of this. Librarians do not agree with D. H. Lawrence that "a book that is a book flowers once, and seeds, and is gone. First editions or forty-first are only the husks of it."[17] Every book contains many seeds which can germinate only in the hands of readers. Every work and every edition of that work is important, and it is important to distinguish each edition. If it is true, as R. W. Chapman says, that "the history of a text is the gradual accretion of error,"[18] then the librarian must know from which text he is serving his public. A retrieval system is no better than its ability to discover textual purity; the definitive edition is usually the one sought. Thompson tells us that even the ancients counted lines,

16

in both prose and poetry, for this purpose.[19] Carter
tells us that the texts of the Confucian Classics and the
Buddhist canon were cut in stone to insure purity.[20]
Bibliographic description and its successor, cataloging,
are a vital part of our history.

The housing of library collections is one of today's
great controversies. Architect, librarian and donor are
never in complete accord. If we consider the building
as a monument and ornament, then the historical line
fades far back into antiquity. Even the earliest public
library buildings were raised to someone's glory, with
the accent on how they looked rather than on how they
served. However, there is evidence from Assurbanipal's library to suggest an awareness of the need for
organized arrangement and we feel sure our beloved
Callimachus and Cassidorus must have paid some attention to proper housing. The first formal attention to
a "library architecture" appears to have been the Avis
of Naudé, in the 1600's. Boulée is credited with the
first attempt, in the late eighteenth century, to fit architecture to the library and its public, and Delessert
is credited with the first of the famous circular reading rooms, which he designed to separate readers from
storage. Modular design is our latest attempt to solve
the housing problem. Our most visible mistakes have
been in architectural design; we should chart our past
errors and study them well.

The administration of personnel and the technical
organization and administration of libraries have received relatively little study. Indeed, conscious classification of library personnel seems to have begun only
in this century, although Adam Smith first published his
principle in 1776. As to organization, the need to
shelve, in the sense of store, and to classify, including
identify and label, seems to have been evident to the
earliest of Keepers, according to both Richardson and
Thompson. They tell of various types of storage practices and devices, each with the purpose to protect, to
identify, to retrieve. Richardson says that, "The putting of like kinds of works in boxes together . . . is
found as early as 2700 B.C. in Egypt and quite early
in Crete. The labels of Crete point to a classification
of objects if not of object records."[21] The great Nin-

17

eveh library used classifying, labeling, catalogs, shelving, colophons, acquisition policies and reprints, and the excellent Pinakes of Callimachus shows a system of organization. The writings extant from the early years of the Christian era provide clues to the attention that was given to rules and regulations for libraries, for librarians and for scriptoria. A personal letter of Theonas, librarian to Diocletian, written sometime between A.D. 282 and A.D. 300, includes his rules for administration of a royal, private library. Humbert of Romans included the matter in his Constitutions. Others, like St. Benedict, Cassiodorus, Columba and Alcuin, wrote out strict and explicit rules for their orders. Thompson says that the Carthusians, founded in 1094, possessed the most advanced methods, in the later Middle Ages, for copying, collecting, registering and even for loans.

We should be interested in the very earliest laws that have affected the discipline. These include the 1537 edict of Francis I and the public library laws of Britain and the United States. We should know the earliest attempts at formal education for librarians (was the first experiment really made in Italy?). We should be concerned with types of censorship and projected legislation (a most intriguing history, running from Tsin Chi Huangti in 213 B.C., through the infamous Sedley case in 1663, to the first attempts at U.S. legislation in 1711 and on to the present), as well as the law of copyright, which destroyed the idea held in Roman times that the "high seas of literature were free to all,"[22] but which brought about that great "right hand" to the national library, the deposit copy.

Why an interest in graphic arts? How important are the illustrations bound in with the text? Are they not just an added bonus? Mallabar, the British bibliographer, says, "Librarians need to study illustration processes. . . . They should be able to assess the value of existing illustrations . . . as to suitability of purpose and faithfulness of reproduction; . . . when ordering . . . be able to select the best process . . . in view of aesthetic suitability, faithfulness, and cost."[23]

Why an interest in mechanical processes and devices? The first known typewriter patent is that of

Mill, in England, 1714. The earliest known proposal
to mechanize the library by use of a typewriter apparently came only in 1877, and this was only a proposal.[24] In 1903, when typing courses were added to the
curriculum at the Albany School, there were strong
voices heard in favor of retaining the courses in handwriting lest the typewriters break down or prove failures! How slow are we, in the library profession, to
recognize a device as useful to us? How willing are
we to aid in its development or adoption?

Why an interest in governments as publishers?
Peter Force says:

> There exist no sources of historical infor-
> mation in a free and enlightened country so
> rich and so valuable as its publick journals,
> and the proceedings and debates of its pub-
> lick bodies and associations.[25]

The rapidly increasing proliferation and ephemeral nature of this source of knowledge make it increasingly
important that libraries collect, preserve and make
these publications available.

Ernest Savage is quoted as saying, "An enthusias-
tic librarian diligently searches for new ideas, but rare-
ly discovers any."[26] Classification schemes, which received so much attention at the end of the nineteenth
century, were not new. Although the need for an elaborate system did not arise until the multiplication of
the printed book, the Chinese used a scheme as early
as A.D. 281, and the first use of symbols in a Western
library was probably at Vivarius, at mid-sixth century.
Reduced size printing, which now claims so much of
our attention, is not new in principle or need. Callimachus is supposed to have preferred small rolls at
the Alexandrian Museum for some of the same reasons
that microprint is employed today: compactness, ease
in use and saving of storage space. It is possible that
the one-inch-long clay tablets of the Chaldeans may be
an even earlier example; certainly the reading instruments discovered with them are progenitors of our reading machines for microreproductions.

Even subscription libraries, which are thought quite

recent as public institutions, have a prototype as early as the second century B.C. Thompson reports that:

> An inscription was found (dating ca. 200-175 B.C.), presumably from the island of Cos, which shows how well-to-do citizens subscribed to the erection of a library building and contributed to a book-purchase fund. [27]

And a prototype of MEDLARS can be found in a proposal for a retrieval program at the British Museum in 1889.

Notes

1. Randolph G. Adams, Three Americanists (Philadelphia: University of Pennsylvania Press, 1939), p. 95.

2. Nineteenth-Century English Books; Some Problems in Bibliography ("Phineas L. Windsor Lectures in Librarianship," No. 3; Urbana, Ill: University of Illinois Press, 1952), p. 50.

3. Adams, p. 95.

4. Ernest Cushing Richardson, The Beginnings of Libraries (Hamden, Conn: Archon Books, 1963), p. 28.

5. Cf. Richardson, pp. 16-47, passim.

6. James Westfall Thompson, Ancient Libraries (Berkeley, Calif: University of California Press, 1940), pp. 1; 14.

7. Edward Alexander Parsons, The Alexandrian Library (New York: The Elsevier Press, 1952), pp. 8-10.

8. Alfred Hessel, A History of Libraries, trans. Reuben Peiss (Metuchen, N.J: Scarecrow Press, 1950), p. 3.

9. Parsons, p. 70.

10. Richardson, p. 20.

11. Information Bulletin (Library of Congress), June 8, 1964, p. 267.

12. Thomas Francis Carter, The Invention of Printing in China, rev. L. Carrington Goodrich (New York: Ronald Press, 1955), p. 238.

13. R. H. Clapperton, Paper and its Relationship to Books (London: J. M. Dent, 1934), p. 9.

14. Dard Hunter, Papermaking through Eighteen Centuries (New York: Wm. Edwin Rudge, 1930), p. 30.

15. Dard Hunter, Papermaking (New York: Knopf, 1943), pp. 3-4. The last named means press printing on paper.

16. Douglas C. McMurtrie, The Book (3d ed.; New York: Oxford University Press, 1943), p. 559.

17. Nineteenth-Century English Books, p. 8.

18. Ibid.

19. Thompson, pp. 72-75.

20. Carter, pp. 20-21.

21. Richardson, p. 149.

22. Thompson, p. 96.

23. Kenneth Aldridge Mallabar, A Primer of Bibliography (London: Association of Assistant Librarians, 1954), p. 73.

24. Cf. Library Trends, V, 2, 194ff.

21

25. John H. Powell, The Books of a New Nation (Philadelphia: University of Pennsylvania Press, 1957), motto.

26. John L. Thornton, The Chronology of Librarianship (London: Grafton, 1949), p. ix.

27. Thompson, p. 24.

Chronological Tables
1st Century

Within this century we can point to important evolutions in areas essential to the development of our concept of acceptable library service: a script and alphabet; an inscribing surface, tool and ink; a book form;
a book trade; and a forerunner to the municipal public
library--plus developments in pictorial illustrating, and
the appearance of an encyclopedia.

About the time of Christ's birth, the Romans had
devised their square capitals for inscriptions on stone
(Glaister p. 223); these form prototypes of our present
upper case letters. With the basis for our lower case
letters laid in 400 A.D. (Roman "current" script) and
600 A.D. (the Irish half-uncial) we theoretically had
our present script; various developments through uncial,
half-uncial, Carolingian (developed by a librarian from
Britain, Abbot Alcuin, while at the Abbey of St. Martin
at Tours), etc. are only extensions. Fabre says
that the Latin [Roman] alphabet has been "particularly
useful in the artificial creation of writing for contemporary peoples [1963] who never developed scripts of
their own"--Fabre p. 36. Chronologically, the story
of our inscribing symbols is: 20,000 B.C., approxi-
mate date of the earliest cave paintings, in northeast
Spain; 3500 B.C., Sumerian pictographic writing, prototype of cuneiform; 3100 B.C., Egyptian hieroglyphics;
2500 B.C., Egyptian cursive hieratic script; 1800-1600
B.C., first real alphabet, Syria-Palestine; 900's B.C.,
Phoenicians transmit above alphabet to the Greeks; 100
B.C., Roman alphabet attains its final form, twenty-
three letters plus Greek y and z, cf. Fabre, "Chronology."

Although parchment appeared as late as the second
century B.C., while papyrus goes back into the antiquity of Egypt (cf. *Thompson, pp. 53; 63), it vied in
use with the latter during this first century, and until

the eighth century A.D., when paper came into the
Western world. Papyrus is reported to have continued
in some use until the eleventh century (Thompson p.
631), but it had disappeared before the beginning of
printing. Parchment lent itself very well to the codex
form and continued in use with the advent of printing,
but when it took the skins of more than three hundred
sheep for a single Bible (DeVinne, p. 41) cheap paper
was destined to take first place. See 105.

Lamb says that as parchment began to displace
papyrus, and as Roman square capitals appeared, the
quill began to displace the reed as a writing tool; he
reports that as early as 150 B.C. the Romans had metal pens for writing, cf. Lamb, passim.

A gall ink is recorded by Philo of Byzantum (Lamb
p. 72); it comes from the gall wasp. Palatino's rec-
ipe for gall ink appears in 1540; Cocker's in 1672; Edward Johnston's in 1927. It is interesting that both
our paper (see year 1719) and our ink should be involved with the wasp!

The codex form for the book is devised
(*Thompson p. 58); a parchment codex, the prototype
of the modern quired, stitched and cut book. It is
through archeology rather than records that the origin
of the codex has been traced, but it was a much needed
reform if today's library service was to be attained.
The codex is easier to store, handle and carry about,
and as Kenyon says, "the codex form afforded a greater convenience of reference and notation"--Kenyon, p.
114. Thompson says that by the sixth century codices
were almost universal (Thompson p. 27).

A retail book shop is recorded as early as 58 A.D.,
in Rome (*Putnam p. 239); about 430 B.C. it would appear that special places were reserved in the market
for book-trade in Greece, but not until Alexander's time
was it developed into any importance; the first literary
quarter or "Grub Street" is reportedly the Kiriath Sepher
assigned to the Hebrew scholars translating the Septua-
gint in Alexandria, ca. 285 B.C.; evidence of a distribution machinery for published literature is found as
early as the first century B.C., perhaps before, in
Rome, as Putnam speaks of Atticus, a publisher of
Rome, 65-35 B.C., and Fabre speaks of the Sosii

24

Brothers, publishers, saying Roman book trade was at the height of its efficiency ca. 100 B.C. (Fabre, "Chronology"); Theodore Birt concludes that leading publishers of Rome had organized an association by the second century A.D.; Fabre reports the foundation of a guild of scribes there as early as 207 B.C. (Fabre, "Chronology"); cf. *Putnam, pp. 102-242, passim. See also year 1472.

A forerunner of the municipal "public" library is dated 92 A.D. (*Thompson p. 35) at ancient Ephesus. It is possible that there were public libraries, as contrasted to private libraries, as early as 500 B.C. We do know that they existed in Roman times, beginning with Asinius Pollio, between 39-27 B.C. Timperley says that the most ancient library on record is that of Asymandyas, King of Egypt, at Memphis, in the time of David, King of Israel (Timperley p. 32); the earliest "public" library is credited to Pisistratus at Athens, 540 B.C. (Fabre, "Chronology").

Illustration, as opposed to decoration, probably began before the Christian era. Bland says the first attempts at actual representation are in the herbals, see also year 1486; Pliny reports there were herbals of the first century B.C. with colored drawings; the earliest one we can date is from the sixth century A.D. (*Bland p. 21); the Chinese ideogram is one of the first forms of illustration with text (picture writing dates from 20,000 B.C.), a combined form; the Egyptian Book of the Dead is the earliest illustrated book to survive; from classical times there are two Virgils and a fragment of the Iliad, showing a fully developed style of illustrating; in medieval times illumination was the only illustration: the miniature; the initial with a scene; drawings in the margins. Our early printed book decorations are most influenced by the Byzantine schools, from that transition period when the Christian world moved eastward. Cf. *Bland, pp. 21-25.

The first encyclopedia of the Christian era is issued in 77 A.D. (Collison p. xiii); Pliny, Historia naturalis; the first known encyclopedia is one by Speusippas, ca. 370 B.C.; in ca. 183 B.C. appeared the first Roman one, by Cato; ca. 50 B.C. appeared the first illustrated encyclopedia, by Varro; ca. 220 A.D. ap-

pears the first Chinese encyclopedia. The encyclopedia
is the king of our reference tools, with the dictionary,
especially the encyclopedic type, as heir presumptive.

100's

100   A Chinese dictionary bears the date January 29,
100 (Carter p. 96); it is block-printed in 986. Diction-
aries trace their origin to the glossary (see 725); about
1225, Johannes de Garlandia probably first used the
term dictionarius, for his collection of Latin vocables,
cf. Glaister, p. 105.

105   Paper is made from rags in China (*Clapperton
p. 1). This is the acceptable date at present for the
first usable rag paper; there seems to have been a
quasi-paper in China before 105, between the silk and
paper eras, cf. Tsien.

175   The earliest probable "reprints" (mass production) are made (Carter p. 20); the text of the Confucian
Classics is cut in stone to insure permanency and ac-
curacy; it is possible that rubbings or "reprints" were
made; the earliest date that can be set with certainty
for a rubbing from an inscription is 627.

180   The earliest reported Christian library is the
one at Alexandria in the reign of Commodus, 180-192
(Thompson p. 15); there may have been one as early
as 177 A.D. One is reported at Jerusalem under Bsp.
Alexander between 212-250 (cf. Thornton, p. 146); and
another at Caesarea before 254; Jerome mentions a
"lending library" of about 30,000 volumes at Caesarea,
begun by Pamphilus, the presbyter, before 309 A.D.,
cf. *Timperley, p. 38.

300's

392   St. Jerome prepares his De illustribus viris, a
list of church writers and their works, an attempt at
a true bibliography (Besterman p. 4); in 480 Gennadius
continues the work and greatly improves the bibliogra-

26

phy; the only bibliography of any note before this seems to be the auto-bibliography of Galen in the second century.

400's

400   This is the earliest possible date for the Roman "current" script, the basis for the miniscules which are the prototypes of our lower case letters (Glaister p. 224).

400   The earliest reported newspaper is that one founded by Tin Kwang Tsing in China about this date (Labarre p. 40); it is cut in wood and "printed" by rubbings. The Acta of Julius Caesar was also a news medium, see 1663. The forerunners of our modern newspapers begin in the handwritten newsletters of European trading companies 1500-1556, cf. Fabre, "Chronology." A popular anecdote tells us that in ca. 1550 a Venetian publisher charged a gazetta for his newspaper, ergo the term gazette in journalistic parlance!

400   A true printing ink is made from lamp black for brush writing and wood-block printing in China (+Hunter p. 313). However, it is not usable for printing from metal (see 1100), cf. Carter; Tsien. Stick ink was known in China by 2697 B.C., in Egypt by 2500 B.C., in Greece by 2200 B.C., cf. Lamb.

450   Actual printing from an incised stamp with a true ink, upon paper, is made in China, using seals (+Hunter, p. 314). This insured exact reprints and greater possibilities for mass production.

496   Censorship: Pope Gelasius issues a decree declaring certain books were not to be read (Glaister, p. 189). Tsin Chi Huangti declared a censorship and destruction of all literature, except that dealing with medicine, agriculture or science, in 213 B.C.; he even executed or banished the authors of the censored works, cf. *Downs, p. 2.

520   The Monastery of Clonard is established (Langer
p. 169); it is reported that 3,000 students live in separate, wattled huts, to learn and dispense knowledge;
from here the Twelve Apostles of Ireland go out to
found schools in Ireland and on the Continent. In such
centers recorded knowledge, the library's stock-in-
trade, is preserved between the era of the Roman library and the revival of the library in Europe.

529   St. Benedick establishes Monte Cassino in Italy
(EB ed. 11, v. 16, p. 573); another center for preserving knowledge, and of the added importance to
libraries for leaving instruction on need for and care
of books in similar institutions. The Pinakes of Callimachus may be the first written work on library organization, although the library of Assurbanipal at Nin-
eveh shows results of a formal plan. Sometime between 282-300 A.D. Theonas, librarian to Diocletian,
writing a personal letter, included his rules for library
management; cf. Wormald, p. 78; the Carthusians,
founded 1094, are reported to have possessed the most
advanced methods of management, cf. Thompson, pp.
311; 390-391.

550   Cassiodorus presents his Institutiones divinarum
(Hessel p. 13). This Roman is important to libraries
for his devotion to the production and care of books for
the preservation of Western culture; with him is to be
classed Aiden at Lindisfarne ca. 635, and Benedict Bis-
cop in England ca. 674.

563   St. Columba founds Iona in Scotland, another center for copying manuscripts and preserving recorded
knowledge (Langer p. 169). Columba is responsible
also for the monasteries of Durrow, Kells and Derry
in Ireland.

597   The mission of St. Augustine is established in
Britain; it means the re-establishment of literacy in
England (Irwin pp. 71-72). "The historian of libraries
must note the evidences of literacy, particularly in

28

periods when it is developing from the mere ability to read, to the formation of the habit of reading; . . ."
--*Irwin, p. 197.

600's

600   In this year the collection of texts of the Buddhist Canon was first cut on stone steles (Carter p. 21), an early program for retrieval and mass reproduction by means of "reprints" from rubbings; it also insured textual purity for the future.

600   The Irish half-uncial appears (Glaister p. 200); another ancestor of our lower case roman letters.

668   A revival of classical studies in England is brought about through the establishment this year of a school and library at Canterbury (Wormald p. 140); Theodore of Tarsus, a learned Greek, arrives as Archbishop of Canterbury, accompanied by Hadrian, a North African abbot, cf. Irwin, pp. 72-74.

700's

700   By this date, incised printing from wooden blocks has appeared in China (Glaister p. 29).

700   The earliest known catalog of a Western library, the Gesta abbatum Fontanellensium at Fulda, dates from this century, cf. Thompson.

725   The Corpus Glossary, a collection of over 2,000 lemmata or words, is issued in England (Glaister p. 155).   This form of reference book can be traced to the fourth century B.C., in Greece; the bilingual ones trace to the 500's A.D.; the English glossed in Latin or Anglo-Saxon and issued glossorium such as this famous one, cf. Glaister.

731   The Bede, Ecclesiastical History of Britain is issued (Besterman p. 3); it is a forerunner of classified bibliography.   The Divine Bede is credited with being the first writer to give attention to citations, i.e.

29

credit to those he quoted.

753   Paper is reported to be made at a mill at Samarkand (Labarre p. 42); the process for making it has been brought out of China by the Caliphs; it will spread westward into Europe, possibly via Egypt and Moorish Spain. See also 1150.

800's

800   The earliest recognizable title page is found in a manuscript of this date (McKerrow p. 88); it is a <u>Gospels</u> in Latin, Harley MS 2788; the title page information appears on the verso of the twelfth leaf, and answers the definition of a true title page: one which gives all information about the book with none of the text.   Weitemeyer reports evidence of a title page was found on the wax tablets discovered at the British excavations at Nimrud (near the ancient capital of Assurbanipal at Calah), cf. <u>Libri</u>, v. 6, no. 3 (1956), p. 233.

831   The catalog of the Benedictine house of St. Requier is issued (Strout p. 9); it uses author entries and shows "collation" and "contents notes."

868   The earliest known block-print book, the <u>Diamond Sūtra</u>, appears (Carter p. 21); a pictorial printing from wood blocks, it exists in a rubbings edition also.   Hunter says that the first printed edition was in 1157, in Japan.   Blum reports that the first efforts to cut pictures on wood blocks are dated 883, cf. *Blum, p. 68.

900's

932   The earliest known mass-production printing program begins this year in the work of printing the <u>Nine Classics</u> and their commentaries under the National Academy, China, cf. Carter, p. 72.

932   The earliest reported government printing office is in the later T'ang Dynasty under Fêng Tao, minister in charge of the National Academy and its program to print the <u>Nine Classics</u>, cf. Carter, p. 95.   See above.

935   Wu Chao-i begins a printing program in China
and is credited with being the first person to use the
art of printing as a means to make literature available
to the common people, cf. Carter pp. 69; 84.

949   The Buddhist sūtra appears, a book form between
the roll and cut pages (Carter p. 58); it is a folded book
of eight pages, block-printed on one side only, pasted
to open like a modern book, but with the bolt unopened,
and with the name of the printer and the date on the
inside of the outer leaf, like a modern imprint. Hunter
sets the date of its earliest appearance as 950.

978   The earliest known book of modern dimensions
(Clapperton p. 16); it measures 8 x 5.5 x 1.4 inches,
an Arabic grammar, D͡iw͡ânu l'-âd͡âb, 289 pages, gatherings irregular.

1000's

1041   The earliest possible date for movable type from
clay, in China (Carter p. 212). These types, cut in
clay and baked, were devised sometime between 1041-
1049; the "type-plate" was set up in wax on iron; about
1314 types were cast in tin, the form being made of
strung iron wire; the multi-character nature of Chinese
writing militated against the use of movable type [inter-
estingly, it has taken photo-set to solve the problem at
LC (see 1959)] cf. McKerrow. DeVinne says that "movable type" is suggested by both Cicero and St. Jerome,
cf. DeVinne, p. 50.

1100's

1100   A forerunner of the oily ink required in press-
printing is devised (McMurtrie p. 129); Theophilus's
directions to mix colors with linseed oil.

1100   An Arabic numeral system is introduced in this
century; Adelard of Bath translates into Latin the Arabic
work of Al-Khwarizmi, introducing the Arabic numeral
system to the Western world in the early twelfth century; it aids the librarian by simplifying pagination, ci-

tation, and indices, cf. Wormald; EA, ed. 1963.

1109　The earliest extant paper document in Europe is accepted to be the deed of King Roger of Sicily, written in Arabic and Latin (Carter p. 137).

1116　The earliest known stitched books appear in this year (+Hunter p. 318); printed on one side, with "French fold, " sewed with linen and cotton thread. Putnam says that Antiphanes (b. 408 B. C.) is credited by Suidas as referring to books "sewed and glued, " cf. *Putnam, p. 103.

1150　Paper is reportedly first made in Europe at Xativa (Carter p. 136); the mill is in Spain in Saracen hands; the first mill in Christian hands is founded in 1157 by Jean Montgolfier at Vidalon in France.

1170　A forerunner to our charging systems possibly may be found in the Christ Church, Canterbury, catalog issued this year (Wormald pp. 23-24); the letter and number on the recto of the first leaf may have been used in a charging system.

1200's

1212　The anathemas on book lending are annulled and loans encouraged in the city of Paris by its Council (Thompson p. 627).

1221　Censorship: Emperor Frederick II forbids the use of paper for public documents (Carter p. 137).

1250　The earliest known example of cooperative cataloging is ascribed to the Registrum Librorum Angliae begun this year (Thornton p. 150). Gordon R. Williams, director of the Center for Research Libraries (MILC), speaking at the SLA conference in 1964, says that this quotation, "man cooperateth with man unto repentence, " from Bishop Ussher of Armagh in 1625, is the first English use of the term cooperate; however one interprets that, cooperative ventures in the twentieth century are felt to be the "redemption" of library service.

1260 Somewhere around this date Humbert of Romans, general of the Dominicans, prepared his Constitutions, with its details on the obligations of the librarian and the care of books (Wormald p. 78).

1266 The Roger Bacon classification system is issued (Thornton p. 151). The need for an elaborate system of classification did not arise until the multiplication of printed books; Richardson says that as early as 2700 B.C. the Egyptians were putting like kinds of works in boxes together, cf. Richardson, p. 149; the Chinese show use of a system as early as 281 A.D.; Cassiodorus at Vivarium (ca 550) probably used the first classification symbols in a Western library, cf. *Irwin.

1276 The Fabriano paper mill appears at Montifano, Italy (Blum p. 22). See also Carter, p. 137.

1282 The earliest known paper with watermarks appears this year; the marks + and o are used (+Hunter p. 320). Herdeg says at Bologna (Herdeg p. 5). In 1794, the Act 34 George III makes it necessary that British-made paper bear the dated watermark in order to collect the draw-back in export duties, cf. Library, ser. 4, v. 25, p. 71.

1289 The library of the Sorbonne is formally organized (Thornton p. 31). It was a gift from Robert de Sorbon in his will dated 1274, cf. Thompson, pp. 255-256. There is evidence that books were provided before this date, see 1320.

1298 This is the earliest possible date for the use of wooden movable type (Carter p. 221). Such type in the Urger language has been dated to 1300, cf. +Hunter.

1300's

1309 Paper is reportedly first used in England (Carter p. 139). It is not yet manufactured there, see also 1492.

1311   The earliest dated portalano (sea charts) are issued this year by Petrus Vesconte (Glaister p. 323) in
a collected or atlas form.   Map origins disappear into
antiquity, but probably are our earliest form of reference tool.   Map-making was also an ancient art, first
in the mind, then drawn on the sand (in the Marshall Is-
lands maps were found made with sea shells and a framework of palm-leaf ribs); clay and papyrus made it possible to make maps with text, cf. Mason, pp. 1-15.
The earliest original map is the mosaic found at Meda-
ba, showing the city before Islam; meridians and parallels come into use in the third century B.C.; modern
cartography begins in the twelfth century A.D.; the use
of "contours" first appears in 1728.   Copyright acces-
sions at LC for 1964 show an expanded production of
cruising charts and guides, today's protalano, cf. Quart.
J v. 22, no. 3.

1320   The chained library in England seems to date
from this year (Thornton p. 152).   Thompson says
there is no evidence of the practice before the thirteenth century except for service books; the first general
use seems to be at the Sorbonne, when in 1271 the gift
of Gerard of Abbeville included the request for chaining,
cf. Thompson.   See also 1799.

1348   The national library, The State Library at Prague,
begins in the Charles University Library at this date
(Esdaile p. 274); it becomes a public library in 1782;
in 1959 it becomes an association of four libraries:
Charles University, the National Library (ca 1930), Sla-
vonic Library (1924), and The Central Economic Library.
The Greeks are supposed to have founded a "state library, " or national library at Heracleia on the Black
Sea before 350 B.C., or at least a hundred years before
the Alexandrian Library, cf. Bushnell, p. 13.   Certainly
all royal libraries were in a sense national libraries,
which makes their origin go very far back.

1370   This is the earliest possible date for printing
from movable type in Europe (Glaister p. 88); the Cos-
teriana or editions of Latin grammars (Aelius Donatus)
attributed to Lourens Janszoon Coster of Haarlem,

"printed" between 1370-1400 in Holland; tradition is the only proof.

1370   The earliest dated carrels in England are the stone "carrells" of Gloucester Cathedral (Clark p. 89); wooden ones are mentioned as early as 1258 for Westminster Abbey, and again in 1327, for Bury St. Edmunds.

1389   A forerunner to modern cataloging is found in the catalog for St. Martin's Priory at Dover, issued this year (Strout p. 11). It has three parts, including analytics, with arrangement by call number, cf. Wormald.

1392   Type is cast from metal in Korea (McKerrow p. 266); fonts are cast in 1403; 1420; 1434; a government type-foundry is established in 1403, which may be the very first type-foundry.   These metal types may have been cast as early as 1232; earliest extant book printed from movable type is dated 1397, cf. Carter, pp. 250; 224.

1394   The catalog prepared this year for Leicester Abbey is reported to be a subject as well as an author one (Thornton p. 155).

1400's

1400   The literacy of the lay population of England advances greatly during this century (Wormald p. 5); Irwin says the lay population becomes a literate society, see also item under 597.   Bryant, Modern English and Its Heritage, says that the language is in its second period.   Many great academic centers are founded, including All Souls, Kings, Queens, Eton.

1400   A forerunner to our modern catalog is found in one for Tichfield, England, issued this year (Wormald p. 25); it gives an arrangement of the library and a brief guide to location; the books are marked outside and on the first folio, suggesting a "call" number.

1400   Sometime within this century a monk reached into his headband, extracted a leather thong and marked his

35

place in the manuscript he was using; Thompson reports this as the first bookmark, cf. Thompson, p. 623. This is much more believable and acceptable than the story we keep hearing about finding a strip of bacon in a returned book!

1402　The forerunner of the circulating library, the "rental" library, is found at Bath, England (Irwin p. 24); the churchwardens are lending out books from the parish library at two-pence per volume. Altick reports that in 1661 the first advertising appears in England, of books "to be read for reasonable considerations, " cf. Altick p. 59. See also 1726. Shera and Thompson say that Paris booksellers lent books for fees, regulated by the universities, to students as early as 1342, cf. Shera, p. 130. Thompson reports that the University of Bologna, as early as 1259, used regulations to protect the students when using the lending services of the city publishers, cf. Thompson, p. 638.

1410　A forerunner of our modern Union Catalog is found in the Catalogus scriptorum ecclesiae of John Boston of Bury (Irwin p. 107). Based on Registrum, it lists 673 authors with biographical details, cf. Besterman; Thornton.

1412　A "chaplain" is designated for the library at Oxford (Predeek p. 21); later Thomas James, "Bodley's librarian, " bore the intriguing title protobibliothecarius Bodleianus. The office of librarian was established at the papal library as early as 772; it is mentioned at Bobbio in 845, cf. Thompson, pp. 46; 139-140.

1412　The earliest reported use of the system of cross references occurs in a catalog prepared by Amphonius Ratnick de Berka (Strout p. 12). In 1943 cross referencing reaches its heights in the U.S. with the LC Subject Heading List beginning its system of x and xx references, cf. Tauber, p. 162.

1423　The oldest surviving dated specimen of the European block-printed book, the St. Christopher (+Hunter p. 321). Carter says the earliest were between 1440-1450;

36

Schreiber says not before 1460; Kristeller and Hind say by 1440, maybe as early as 1425; McMurtrie says there are forerunners as early as 1350; Blum says a <u>Virgin</u> dated 1418 may be authentic, and he dates the <u>Protat</u> block at 1370 or 1380, cf. Carter; McMurtrie; *Blum.

1436 A forerunner of the public library-by-bequest is that of Noccolo Niccoli, Italy, who is reported to have left a library of 800 volumes for the use of the public (EB ed. 11, v. 16, p. 551). Petrarch's bequest of 1352 is doubted by most experts, but the report of Pisistratus' bequest to Athens, ca 527 B.C., may be true, though one may ask "what public?".

1440 Gutenberg has begun his experiments with movable type (Steinberg p. 21). The lawsuit of 1439 indicates this, cf. McMurtrie, p. 139.

1444 The Waldfoghel claim to the art of artificial writing is set in this year (Estienne p. 4); a jeweler of Prague claims to have the <u>ad scribendum artificialiter</u>, with two alphabets in steel, two in iron, one iron vise or press, forty-eight forms in pewter and various other forms.

1448 An astronomical calendar may have been printed at Mainz in this year (Haebler p. 38).

1450 The earliest reported use of a bookplate, an "ex libris," to show ownership, one printed on paper and pasted in (+Hunter p. 322). Winship says that the earliest known bookplate as sign of ownership may be older than typography; he reports a block-printed one for a Hans Igler, undated, cf. Winship, p. 71.

1450 The earliest reported use of calfskin (calf) book binding is in this year (Glaister p. 52). There is a remote origin to bookbinding in the leather or board covers used on Roman block-books; except in the sense of decorative case or protective container, binding was not an art, nor a practice, until after press printing, cf. Thompson.

1450 The Vatican library is reported to be formed by
Pope Nicholas V, (*Steinberg p. 97). There already existed a collection of books; Thompson says that Cassiodorus and Agapetus collected some works which may
have become the nucleus of the Pope Gregory library;
between 590-604 Gregory the Great established a small
library; in 649 the works were removed from a papal
library to the papal archives; between 741-752 Pope
Zacharias built a special place for the works, cf. Thompson.

1454 The "first piece of printed matter showing efficient use of the invention of movable types, which can
be dated with certainty" (McKerrow p. 268); the Indul-
gences of Nicholas V, from the press of Johann Gutenberg.

1455 Gutenberg's presses and type pass to Fust &
Schoeffer (Steinberg p. 22). It is in 1465 that they use
the term multiplicare in the sense of reproducing a text
in a multiple fashion and without limit (in their St.
Augustine De arte predicondi); mass production of books
did indeed seem to have arrived.

1456 The Vulgate Bible (the Mazarine), the 42-line Bible,
is completed at the press, before August 15 (McKerrow
p. 268).

1457 The earliest reported use of a colophon in a
printed book (*Esdaile p. 101); a Psalter done by Fust
& Schoeffer in which printing is proclaimed an art distinct from manuscripts, cf. Haebler, p. 98. Weitmeyer
reports that evidence of a colophon was found on the
tablets of pictorial writing discovered at Fara; it gives
title, series, catchline, scribe's and owner's names, cf.
Libri, v. 6, no. 3, p. 226.

1457 The earliest reported use of printed colored initials, the work done without service of the rubricator
(Pollard p. 3); in the Psalter of Fust & Schoeffer. In
1471 wood-cut initials to be hand colored, or straightly
hand-colored ones, were popular, and the "director,"
used by scribes to indicate the wanted initial, begins to

be a printed instruction in printed books, cf. Pollard, p. 25.

1458 The earliest reported pulling of proof sheets from a press is in this year (Glaister p. 151). This is a forerunner of the old "galley proofs," the first of which are reported by Savage as of 1841, and which have now passed almost into oblivion because of "proofing" processes before the first printing.

1458 The first examples of "paste prints," a form of illustration on book binding, are reported this year (Glaister p. 302).

1460 The Catholicon is printed by Gutenberg (Steinberg p. 22); its typographic importance lies in its economical use of smaller types. Already "reduced printing" has presented itself as a factor. McMurtrie says that Froben printed a Latin Bible in 1491 which used type of a reduced size, cf. McMurtrie, p. 306. Irwin reports that Cassiodorus had a Jerome Bible copied in a "small hand" to shorten the length of the textual portion of the manuscript, cf. *Irwin, pp. 100-101. See also 1500; 1934.

1461 The generally accepted first printed book to use printed illustrations is reported produced by Pfister this year (Glaister p. 441). The Boner, Edelstein has spaces left for illustrations to be impressed by hand, cf. The Dance of Death. Blum reports that Pfister published an Ackermann von Bohmen with a probable date of 1460, cf. *Blum, p. 142.

1462 Schoeffer is reported to have first used his device, suspended shields, in the colophon to his Biblia Latina (Pollard p. 25); this is reported as the first use of a printer's device, no other being known until about 1470. Modern publishers' devices are an outgrowth of this idea. See also 1539.

1463 The accepted first printed title page is that of Fust & Schoeffer for their Bull of Pius II (McKerrow p. 89). In 1470, Arnold ther Hoernen is reported to have used a whole page for his "title" for the Sermo ad populum published at Cologne, a step closer to our modern conception of this part of a book. The custom of printing a short "label title" on the first page of a book begins on the Continent and in England around 1490. Glaister says Machlinia used such in his A passing gode lityll boke, ca 1489; Pollard says Wynkyn de Worde used it too, about the same time. The first ornamented title pages are reported as those of the editions of the Calendar of Ratdolt, published in Venice in 1476 and 1478; of more importance they carry "imprint" and "title" on the same page; the title page as we use it (author, title, full imprint) appears about 1520, cf. Pollard; Glaister; Esdaile. The first reported engraved title page, from copper-plate, done in England, is the one for Thomas Germini, Compendiosa totius anatomiae delineatia published in London, 1545 (Glaister p. 85). The now familiar half-title page or "bastard title" appears in the mid-seventeenth century, cf. *Carter, p. 109.

1465 The earliest reported type for Greek letters is that used at Subiaco for a Lactantius of October 29, this year (McKerrow p. 270).

1465 The earliest reported mention of blotting paper is in this year (Sutermeister p. 12); a coarse grey product probably in use early in the century. Garnett speaks of a minor invention, serviceable to bookmen, in use in Italy in the seventeenth century--blotting-paper; Sutermeister quotes from a 1519 text, "Blottyng papyr serveth to drye weete wrytyngs, lest there be made blottis and blurris"; Mann says it was not generally accepted as a drying-agent until the nineteenth century.

1466 The earliest reported use of a printed advertisement of books is issued by Heinrich Eggestein of Strasbourg (Glaister p. 2), an early form of trade bibliography. Putnam tells us that the authors of Rome, in the first century, prepared advertising for booksellers in the form of epigrams, giving format, price, and place of purchase, cf. *Putnam, p. 218. It is also reported that advertising was pasted on the doorways to the booksellers' shops.

1467 A forerunner of the modern "pictorial editions" is reported in the Ulrich Han production of the Torquemada, Meditations (Dance of Death p. v); the woodcuts are reproductions of the actual pictures in Santa Maria sopra Minerva, Rome, the first known ones of existing objects, not artistic fancies. See also 1486.

1467 The earliest reported cutting of roman type is at Strasbourg this year (Steinberg p. 32); it is brought to perfection by Nicolas Jensen, at Venice in 1470.

1468 The earliest recorded miniature book is the Diurnale Maguntinum printed by Schoeffer (McMurtrie p. 308); it measures 2.5 x 3.75 inches, type page, and is extant in two leaves only.

1469 A forerunner to trade bibliography is in a printed prospectus outlining a projected work, issued by Mentelin at Strasbourg (Glaister p. 331). Schoeffer is reported to have issued a trade list this year also, cf. Besterman.

1469 The earliest reporting of a "copyright" is to John of Spira in this year (Putnam p. 15); it was given by the Senate of Venice as the exclusive right for five years to print certain works. Putnam further reports that Darus the librarius, at the time of Seneca, became one of the earliest buyers of publication rights, cf. *Putnam, p. 244; he also reports an early record of rights of literary property in 1486, and a case of the transferring of privilege to another in 1493, cf. +Putnam, v. 2, p. 345.

1469 The earliest reported specimen sheet (type) is issued by Fust & Schoeffer (Glaister p. 381); in 1486 Ratdolt issues an interesting one; in 1665 the first English one is issued by Nicholas Nicholls; in 1734 William Caslon issues his very famous one; in 1567 the earliest known specimen book is issued by Christopher Plantin; in 1763 Caslon issues the first such English book. See

41

also Updike, pp. 93-95.

1470   A forerunner of the "table of contents" is in the
use of a registrum in the Epistolae Hieronymi (Hain
8550) published this year (Haebler p. 55).   Collison
says that thorough indexing reaches back only about one
hundred years (from 1964), cf. Collison; and he says
further that the eighteenth century saw the first real attempts at indexing, e.g. Cruden's Concordance, 1737,
first grand scale indexing, cf. *Collison, pp. 16-22.

1470   Arnold ther Hoernen, Cologne, uses a whole page
for the "title" to his Sermo ad populum (Pollard p. 30);
probably the first title page of this nature.   See also
1463.

1470   The earliest recorded "book salesmen" are the
Buchhändler of South German cities, reported in this
year (Estienne p. 26).

1470   The earliest known use of foliation or leaf numer-
als in the printed book is ascribed to John of Spira at
Venice in this year (Glaister p. 143).

1470   Pollard reports that Arnold ther Hoernen, at Cologne, uses the first pagination in printed books in 1470
and 1471 (Pollard p. 35).   In 1494 the first English
printed book using pagination is reportedly done by Pynson in his Opus grammatices, numbered pagina prima,
pagina ii, etc.; about 1570 it was more frequently used;
after 1590 it appears more often than foliation, cf. Mc-
Kerrow, p. 86.   Haebler has reported that the first
pagination used by Aldus Manutius was in 1499, at Venice, in his Perottus, Cornucopiae (Hain 12706), cf.
Haebler, p. 72.

1471   The earliest reported use of catchwords in printed books is ascribed to this year, at Ferrara (McKerrow p. 83).   Putnam reports the use of catchwords on
the clay tablets of the Chaldeans, cf. *Putnam, p. 151.

1472   The earliest reported printed signatures are ascribed to Koelhoff at Cologne, in his Preceptorium di-

vinae legis of Nider (McKerrow p. 75).

1472   The earliest beginning of printed border decoration in printed books is ascribed to Zainer's wood-cut
initials with trailing vines (GWK 1292) done at Augsburg
this year (Glaister p. 43).   Pollard reports that Sensen-
schmidt introduced illustrations into the large initials of
a Bible printed at Nuremberg this year; Zainer is reported to have used them in 1473 and 1477.

1472   The first attempts are made to print initials in
black like the text, at the same time as the text (Haebler p. 113); an early effort to free the printer from
the rubricator.   See also 1473.

1472   The earliest reported publishing company is organized at Milan (Steinberg p. 92); there is a policy
board, composed of a priest, schoolmaster, professor,
lawyer, doctor and printer, to select books and fix
prices.   See also item under 1st century.   There was
a book trade in the Roman world but it disappeared after the "fall"; during the Middle Ages there is little
evidence except in Italy; industrial book making begins
with the rise of the academic centers in the twelfth century; by 1140 trade was on a business basis in Paris,
cf. Thompson, p. 636; 643.   Steinberg reports that the
first true publisher, one who did not print his own
stock, was Johann Rynmann (d. 1522) of Augsburg, cf.
Steinberg, pp. 92-93.   Putnam says the practice of as-
sociating a work with the name of its publisher began
with the printed book; Winship says that only after 1600
did the publisher dominate the other craftsmen, i.e.
master printers, pressmen, etc.

1473   The earliest known "best-seller" is ascribed to
Zainer's edition of the Imatato Christi (Steinberg p. 102).
Thompson says the endless series of lives of saints,
issued beginning about 365 A.D. and read as novels are
today, were the first "best-sellers, " cf. *Thompson, p.
26.

1473   The earliest reported all-printed book is ascribed
to Zainer's De regimine principum (Pollard p. 35); it is

untouched by the rubricator, having printed headlines, chapter headings, paragraph marks, large and small initials; the printer has freed himself from the hand craftsman. See also 1472.

1473   The earliest of the book fairs are reported to begin at Frankfort, Germany, this year (AmLA 1961, p. 169).

1473   The Philobilon of Richard de Bury (Richard Aungerville of Bury St. Edmunds) is issued in its first printed edition (Glaister p. 49); Bury is an early benefactor of the "public" library, having founded one at Oxford open to all students. See also 1484.

1474   Caxton's first book is published, at Bruges, his translation of Le Recueil des Histories de Troyes of Raoul le F'evre, in 700 folio pages (Steinberg p. 159).

1476   The earliest reported English printing press is ascribed to William Caxton, at Westminster (Glaister p. 63).

1476   The earliest reported use of copper engravings to illustrate a printed book is ascribed to Mansion at Bruges, in his edition of Boccaccio, Du Dechiet des Nobles Hommes et Femmes (Glaister p. 85).   Bland says the processes of copper engraving were undoubtedly known before the time of printing, but wood-cuts were simple and cheaper to use and the former were not generally used for book illustrating until the end of the sixteenth century, cf. *Bland, p. 30.

1476   The earliest known real music printing is ascribed to Ulrich Han at Rome, in his Missale Romanum (Haebler p. 135); a five-line staff in red with square notes in black.

1476   Erhard Ratdolt prints a Calendario at Venice which has the "imprint" and the "title" on the same page (Glaister p. 188).   Probably the first title page of that nature.   See also item on title pages under 1463.

1476   The first reported "blurb" (McMurtrie p. 562).
It was a verse eulogizing the work, which suggests that
many colophons or explicits were "blurbs."

1477   The earliest known English printed book to bear a
date is ascribed to Caxton's Dictes or Sayingis of the
Philosophres (Glaister p. 63).

1477   The earliest reported printed book to use intaglio
printed illustrations is ascribed to the Il Monte Santo di
Dio, printed at Florence (Glaister p. 195).

1477   The earliest known engraved maps, printed from
copper plates, are ascribed to a Ptolemy, Cosmographia done at Bologna (Glaister p. 249); authorities have
disagreed on the date.   The Rosenwald collection at LC
reports a Ptolemy with copperplate maps issued 1477,
cf. Quart. J v. 22, no. 3, p. 175.

1477   Caxton prints Ordinalis sarum with the earliest
known advertising handbill in English printing history.
(Steinberg p. 74).   This forms another piece of early trade
bibliography.

1478   The Oxford University Press is established and publishes its first book (Sears p. 1).   Putnam reports that the
first printing press at Paris, 1469, was university sponsored and the first book printed in 1470 bore the imprint in
aedibus Sorbonnae, cf. +Putnam, v. 1, p. 167. Similarly,
the first known press in the Colonial period of U.S. history was "university" sponsored, when Harvard housed the
Daye Press.

1478   The earliest known use of fleuron in decorative
printing is ascribed to the Aluise at Verona, in their
Arte de ben marire (Hain 4398) printed this year (Glaister p. 139).

1479   The first known trade catalog of books for sale is
issued by Anton Koberger, at Nuremberg (Estienne p.
16).

1481   The earliest reported illustrated printed book in
England is the Mirrour of the World, a popular encyclo-

pedia printed by Caxton (Glaister p. 63).

1482   The earliest reported maps from woodcuts, in a printed book, are ascribed to Leonhard Holl, at Ulm, in his Ptolemy Cosmographia, edited by Germanus (Pollard p. 49).

1482   Ratdolt is reported to do the earliest work with color printing from woodcuts, using up to four colors (Glaister p. 78).   See also 1457.

1482   Ratdolt is reported to issue the first successful printing of mathematical symbols, at Venice (McMurtrie p. 283).

1484   The earliest reported collection of printed books is ascribed to John Shirwood, Bishop of Durham, a collection principally of fine printed volumes purchased at Rome from 1484-1494 (Wormald p. 123).   This constitutes the first serious attention to the new art as a collector's interest, and possibly forms the first collection of incunabula in England.   The first private collector in England is reportedly Richard de Bury, who between 1329-1345 collected about 1500 items as weapons in fighting heresy, cf. Wormald, pp. 113-114.

1485   The earliest known use of blind-stamping on book bindings in England is reported this year (Glaister p. 29).

1485   By this date contemporary writers, as well as the standard authors, are being printed on the presses (McMurtrie p. 320).

1486   A censorship office to control the printing at Mainz is reportedly the first known (Steinberg p. 186); made up of the church and town councils.

1486   An early record of a copyright recognizing the rights of "literary property" is that of granting to Antonio Sabellico, Venice, the right to publish his own work for an indefinite term, with a penalty of five hundred ducats set up (+Putnam, v. 2, p. 345).

46

1486   The earliest known example of color printing of
illustrations in an English printed book is the Book of
St. Albans (Bland p. 138). This is the Juliana Berners,
The Bokys of Hauking and Hunting printed on paper with
colored illustrations, cf. Carter, p. 477.

1486   Another forerunner of the modern "pictorial edition" (see also 1467) appears in the Breydenback and
Reuwich work on a pilgrimage to Jerusalem, termed
now as the first truly topographical book--an attempt to
illustrate at first hand (Bland p. 108).   Pollard says
that in 1484 and 1485 Schoeffer brought out botanical
works which contained some illustrations closely reproducing the plants described, cf. Pollard p. 56.

1486   The Breydenback and Reuwick work on a Jerusalem pilgrimage contained the earliest known "fold-out"
illustrations, maps and drawings, one five-feet long
(Bland p. 108).

1490   The earliest reported use of "running titles" is
in Albertus Magnus' Philosophia pauperum, issued this
year at Brescia (Steinberg p. 109).   Pollard says Arnold ther Hoernen, at Cologne, used the first headlines
in 1470-1471, cf. Pollard, p. 35.

1490   McMurtrie reports a true miniature book produced
this year, a Beatae Mariae Virginis issued by Morevus
at Naples, a sixtyfourmo in 106 leaves, measuring
40mm x 60mm (McMurtrie p. 308).   Spielmann reports
the first English miniature as the Hours of the Blessed
Virgin, printed 1500 by Julius Notary; the first U.S.
miniature as the A Wedding Ring Fit for a Finger, printed in 1700 by T. G. for William Secker (Spielman, Introd.).

1492   Earliest possible date for an English paper mill
(Clapperton p. 17); the Tate mill at Stevenage or Hart-
ford.   Authorities disagree on the exact date, cf. Mc-
Kerrow; Glaister.   Wynkyn de Worde used some of
Tate's paper, which is still preserved in libraries; his
Bartholomaeus Anglicus is celebrated as the first Eng-
lish book printed on English paper, cf. +Esdaile, p. 187.

1493   Earliest reported piece of Americana: the Co-
lumbus letter, on a single sheet, printed at Barcelona
in Spanish, April of this year (Bühler p. 93).

1493   A recognition of the rights of "literary property"
is shown in the granting of "copyright privilege" to
another than the author; Daniela Barharo is granted this
privilege in her deceased brother's work Castigationes
Plinii (+Putnam, v. 2, p. 345).

1494   Pynson is reported to have used the first pagination in an English printed book, in his Opus grammatices, numbered pagina prima, pagina ii, etc. (McKerrow
p. 86). See also 1470.

1494   The Tritheim bibliography Liber de scriptoribus
eccleciasticus is published, the first serious attempt at
a systematic work, using the idea of the "added entry"
(Besterman p. 8).

1498   Aldus Manutius issues a published catalog of his
books for sale, including prices (Steinberg p. 97); later
editions appear in 1503 and 1513. This is a serious
attempt at trade bibliography.

1499   The first detailed report on the art of printing is
issued by Koehlhoff, in the Chronicle of Cologne (Steinberg p. 27).

1500's

1500   Italic type is cut by Francesco da Bologna, known
as Griffi or Griffo, for Aldus Manutius, sometime
around this date (Glaister p. 200). The use of italics
created a revolution in printing method; the compact
form enabled the printer to compose the text into a
smaller number of pages, reducing the cost and the un-
wieldly size. See also 1460; 1934.

1500   The first velvet bindings for English books are
reported to appear this year (Glaister p. 430).

1500   This is the possible date for substituting cardboard for woodboard in bookbinding (Glaister p. 40).

1501 The earliest attempts to extend censorship beyond
mere control of heretical works are reported this year
(Steinberg p. 186).

1501 The first book printed in italics is supposedly a
Virgil, done at the Aldine Press (Glaister p. 200). The
"pocket editions" of Aldus Manutius may have appeared
this year, cf. Fabre.

1502 The first printed almanac in England is ascribed
to Richard Pynson, this year (Glaister p. 6); almanacs
trace their origin to the fasti of ancient Rome; as a
term, almanac appears in Roger Bacon's encyclopedia
in 1267. Carter reports that in 1328 over three mil-
lion Moslem almanacs were issued, in three sizes, with
lucky and unlucky days prophesized, cf. Carter, p. 94.
The first almanacs in the Colonial period of U.S. history were weather forecasts; the Peirce almanack, reported in the Winthrop Journal, seems to be the first
one printed here; the famous Poor Richard's begins in
1732. McMurtrie says the earliest printed "weather report" was one by Gascano at Venice in 1470; no copy
extant, cf. McMurtrie, p. 318.

1503 Possibly the first literary censorship occurs at
Venice in this year, a censorship of all books printed
in Greek (+Putnam, v. 2, p. 356).

1510 The first gothic type is cut by Schoensperger at
Augsburg (Steinberg p. 35).

1510 Daniel Hopfer experiments with engraving plates
made from etched iron (Glaister p. 126).

1513 A forerunner of the news magazine appears in
England (Steinberg p. 168); a 12-page report of the Bat-
tle of Flodden Field under the title The Trewe Encount-
re, printed by Richard Faques at London.

1513 An etching by Urs Graf, a single leaf bearing
this date, may be the first such in the history of etch-

ing (Glaister p. 126).

1514   The first academic foundation of the English Renaissance is said to be a library, the one at Corpus Christi College (Irwin p. 100).

1514   The earliest reported case of an author being paid a publications fee is that of Thomas Murner, a Roman Catholic pamphleteer, for his Geuchmatt (Steinberg p. 152).   However, Putnam says that it seems likely that Roman authors, from the time of Caesar, were able to secure some portion of the proceeds of the sales of their books, cf. *Putnam, p. 224.

1518   The earliest known granting of a copyright in England is reportedly that for Pynson this year; his title page declares cum privilegio (Putnam p. 16).

1518   The first reported English book set in roman type is Richard Pace's Oratio in pace nuperrime composita, printed by Pynson at London (Glaister p. 350).

1518   The earliest dated chiaroscuro engraving appears this year, one by Ugo da Carpi (Glaister p. 78); the chiaroscuro, a wood engraving which uses successive impressions from blocks to secure light and dark shadings, traces its origin to Georg Lucas Cranach, about 1507, cf. Glaister, p. 65.   See also 1642; 1865.

1520   The earliest reported use of catchwords in English printed books is Pynson's use of them in the Thomas More, Epistola ad Germanum Brixium (McKerrow p. 83).   See also 1471.

1521   The Cambridge University Press begins with publishing the Henry Bullock Oration (Glaister p. 54). See also Sears, p. 1.

1524   A censorship of the printed book is instituted in England by an act of October 12 which warns against importing books for sale without showing them to the authorities (Bennett p. 33).   The first list of censored books is reported as of this year, by Charles V, cf.

50

*Downs, p. 2. The Henry VIII censorship on certain books comes in 1526, cf. Glaister, p. 189.

1524   Martin Luther urges the municipal authorities in Germany to use funds not only for grammar schools but also for "book-houses" (Hessel p. 51). This constitutes a bid for "public libraries."

1526   Possibly the first moral censorship of books and reading occurred under the Venice Council of Ten in 1526-1527 (+Putnam, v. 2, p. 257). The first reported English case on obscenity is the famous King v Sir Charles Sedley case in 1663; the first U.S. law concerning obscenity is reported in Massachusetts in 1711; the first obscenity conviction in the U.S. is reported as of 1821, in Massachusetts (involved the Memo of a Woman of Pleasure), cf. *Downs, passim.

1526   The Vienna National Library, the Hofbibliothek, is first referred to in this year (Esdaile p. 77); in the eighteenth century it incorporated with the libraries of the University of Vienna (1364) and the city of Vienna (1466).

1529   The earliest known appearance of an "errata et addenda" is ascribed to Froben in printing a work of Erasmus (Steinberg p. 92). The latter is credited with influencing the use of another term, the manual, a small service book used during Mass because of its convenient size; after Erasmus produced Manual of the Christian Knight, the term becomes generally used for a guide-book on techniques.

1530   The earliest known example of fore-edge painting is the work this year of Thomas Berthelet, binder to Henry VIII (Glaister p. 143); the first dated work with a disappearing fore-edge painting is a 1651 Bible with a painting of the Leigh arms signed 1653.

1537   The earliest known legally enforced depository law is the one enacted in France (Esdaile p. 56); one copy of every book printed in France is to be deposited in the royal library at Blois, and a copy of every book

51

printed abroad and sold in France is to be offered to the library for purchase. Other depository laws, not involved with copyright, come in 1575, Austria; 1661, Sweden; 1697, Denmark; 1699, Germany; 1757, for the British Museum (see also 1610); 1782, Czechoslovakia.

1539   The earliest reported decree to protect a printer's device is instituted in France; Francis I forbids the use of a printer's personal device by another printer or bookseller (Glaister p. 105).

1539   The earliest evidence of printing in Mexico appears this year (Carter p. 250); under the printer Juan Pablos (Giovanni Paoli, his Italian name). McMurtrie says that Estaban Martin may have been the first printer, cf. McMurtrie, p. 393. See also 1639; 1640.

1540   The earliest book to use copper engraved illustrations cut in England, is reportedly the Richard Jonas translation of the German treatise on childbirth, under title Byrth of Mankynde (Glaister p. 85). Pollard tells us that this was Thomas Raynald's work and had four plates of surgical diagrams, which in later editions have been re-engraved on wood; earlier books had copper engravings cut on the Continent; in 1496 Pynson used a device from copperplate probably cut in England, cf. Pollard, pp. 247-248. The earliest known engraved title page cut in England is one for Thomas Germini, at London in 1545, and the earliest known copper engraved maps are the Christopher Saxton county maps of 1574-1579, cf. Glaister.

1543   The printing of Greek letters from movable type is reported to be introduced into England this year by Reynold Wolfe (Thornton p. 163). See also 1465.

1545   The Conrad Gesner Bibliotheca universalis is published, a forerunner of systematic bibliography in its attempts at a classification of knowledge (Besterman p. 15).

1546   John Leland's The Laboryous Journey is presented to Henry VIII (Besterman pp. 21-22); it constitutes the

earliest known attempt at a national bibliography for
England.

1548   The John Bale Illustrium majoris Britanniae scriptorum is issued (Besterman pp. 21-22); the first true
national bibliography for England.

1548   The Gesner classification system is issued this
year (Thornton p. 163).

1550   The Act of 1550 is enacted in England, which
causes destruction and dispersal of the great English
monastic libraries (Irwin p. 97).

1557   The Stationers' Company, England, is incorporated (Steinberg p. 78).   The date may be 1556; this corporation of printer-publishers becomes a powerful force
to stifle free development of the English book trade,
but its registers are invaluable to bibliographers, cf.
Putnam; Thornton.

1558   A forerunner of the practice of "added entry" is
found in the catalog of the Priory of Bretton in York-
shire, which enters works under editors and translators
as well as authors (Strout p. 12).   See also 1494.

1559   The Index Librorum Prohibitorum is first drawn
this year, by Pope Paul IV (*Downs p. 2); it is printed
in 1564.   See also 1524.

1560   The Florian Trefler treatise on library management is published, including a scheme of classification,
the use of call numbers and arrangement for a five-part
catalog (Steinberg p. 13); the five-part catalog includes:
author entry, shelf list, classified index, alphabetical
index to classes, list of books not in the main collection.

1564   A forerunner of the trade catalog is the George
Willer listing of new books for sale at the Frankfort
Fair this year (Glaister p. 147); it was first issued by
the Fair in 1590 (Estienne says 1598).

1579 The earliest known true typefounder in England is Benjamin Sympson, who begins his work this year (Steinberg p. 122).

1579 The proposal that paper replace expensive leather for bookbinding is made by Samuel Zimmerman in his book on technical papermaking (*Hunter p. 22).

1583 The cataloging rules of Grude de la Croix du Maine are issued this year (Dewey ed. 16, Introd.); they are to be an influence on codes in the U.S.

1584 The wall-system of shelving is used at the Escorial, Spain, with the books unchained (Thompson p. 624); this may have been its first serious use in Western libraries; it was introduced in the Bodleian in 1610-1612. The pigeon-holes for the clay tablets of Assurbanipal (Weitemeyer calls them "built-in-bookcases," with niches 25-30cm high and wide by 40-50cm deep), and those later for papyrus rolls must be recognized as "wall-systems" also. Storing books on vertical shelving, spines out, is generally practiced about 1600, cf. Glaister, p. 41. The famous movable presses of Samuel Pepys are done in 1666-1668 and may still be seen at Magdalen College, Cambridge.

1585 The term "atlas" is reportedly first used for a collection of maps bound together by Gerard Mercator in his Atlas sive cosmographicae published at Duisberg 1585-1595 (Glaister p. 13).

1587 The Bodleian Library is established at Oxford by Sir Thomas Bodley, from the old library of the Duke of Gloucester ("Good Duke Humphrey") (Predeek p. 8). The first books for the Duke Humphrey Library are reported as of 1435; the building, 1488, cf. Thompson.

1595 Petrus Bertius produces a printed catalog for the library of the Rijksuniversiteit, Leyden, the first printed one for a general collection (Ranz p. 2); in 1640 a second catalog is issued.

1595 The Andrew Maunsell Catalogue of English Printed Books, issued this year, lays the foundation for descriptive bibliography in England (Steinberg p. 182). Ranz says he used a classified subject arrangement, with author's surnames alphabetical under that, a departure from custom, cf. Ranz, p. 2; Strout, p. 14.

1595   The Bibliothèque Nationale is founded (Thornton p. 166); a continuation of the Bibliothèque du Roi founded by Charles V in 1365.   Pleas to the Crown had already been made in England for a national library: John Dee to Mary I in 1556, and Sir Humphrey Gilbert to Elizabeth I in 1572; Sir Humphrey requests "certain deposit rights" also, cf. Thornton; Wormald.

1595   The earliest known printed English directory is issued this year, for London business houses (Glaister p. 107).

1599   The earliest recorded book auction is reported to be in Holland for the library of Philip von Marnix (Glaister p. 37).

1600's

1600   Georg Henisch's printed catalog for the Bibliotheca Augustana, Augsburg, is published; the second one appears in 1633 (Ranz p. 2).   This is an influential catalog in the history of the printed form, especially for the printed academic catalog.

1601   A "public" library is reported established in a Free Grammar School of Coventry; this and the one at Norwich in 1608 are reportedly the first public libraries in England, cf. Thornton, p. 46.   However, the Guildhall Library, established by the will of Richard Whittington, 1423, is described as a libraria communis, and Richard de Bury was pressing for public libraries at Oxford in the fourteenth century, cf. #Irwin, p. 122; Glaister, p. 49.

1602   The Bodleian Library opens for service, reported to be the first semi-private library in Europe (Glaister p. 36).

1602　The Lipsius De bibliothecis syntagma is published at Antwerp (+Thornton p. 6); earliest known modern history of libraries.

1604　The first true English dictionary, as we know it today, is published; Robert Cawdrey, Table Alphabetical, with some 3000 words (Glaister p. 6). The famous Johnson dictionary appears in 1755; the first Noah Webster in 1806.

1605　The Bodleian Library, under Thomas James, prints the first of the English printed catalogs (Predeek p. 20). In 1620 the second catalog is arranged alphabetically by entry word in one sequence, a first such arrangement; in 1635 a supplement appears; the 1605 catalog is in the first Harvard College collection, cf. Ranz, p. 2.

1605　The Baconian classification scheme is issued this year (Besterman p. 17).

1610　A forerunner of the depository law lies in Sir Thomas Bodley's arrangement with the Stationers' Company to present to the Bodleian a copy of every book printed and published by the members, the first "statutory" or "deposit" copy (Glaister p. 36).

1617　The earliest reported "subscription book," one sold in pre-publication contracts, is the John Minsheu Guide into tongues, privately printed this year (Glaister p. 397). Another is the polyglot Bible printed 1653-1657 by Thomas Roycroft for the Bishop of Chester. The most famous one in our time is the Audubon Birds of America, in the "elephant folio," issued in parts 1827-1838.

1620　The first "public" library in Colonial U.S. is projected for Henrico, Virginia (Shera p. 16); a gift from Thomas Burgrave to the proposed college at Henrico. Although the college did not materialize, some books were collected and the project is claimed as the antecedent of the present Wm. and Mary college, Williamsburg.

1620   The Blaeu Press is reported to be built about this date by Wilhelm Janszoon Blaeu of Amsterdam (Glaister p. 28); a famous old hand press.

1621   The English Corantos, early "newspapers," begin in London under Thomas Archer (Steinberg p. 171).

1625   The marbling of paper is introduced into England through Bacon's treatise, Sylva Sylvarum (Glaister p. 251). It probably was a Persian invention as early as 1550, cf. +Hunter p. 324; however, Glaister says that there was a marbled paper in Japan as early as 800 A.D. Its use as end papers from the middle seventeenth century, and in half-bound and quarter-bound books of the eighteenth and nineteenth centuries, makes it a very familiar type of paper in the U.S., cf. *Carter, p. 131.

1627   A forerunner to modern practices in library management is the Naudé Avis pour dresser une bibliothèque (Wormald p. 11); Irwin says this is the first attempt to produce a systematic textbook on library economy. It is also the first serious discussion of library architecture, although Thompson says that the library as a separate room with its own special furnishings began as early as the twelfth century, cf. Thompson, p. 623.

1627   The earliest reported general atlas to be published in England is the Speed Prospect of the Most Famous Parts of the World (Glaister p. 381).

1629   The first true bibliography of Americana is ascribed to the catalog raissonné of León Pinelo, the Epitome de la Bibliotheca Oriental i Occidental (Bühler p. 96).

1629   A collection of books arrives for a Salem library with a party of Puritans bound for that Bay colony (Shera p. 16); it is only conjecture as to what happened to the books; a part of the collection was a gift from William Backhouse.

1637   The earliest reported bookbinder shop in the Colonies is that of John Sanders at Boston (Lehmann p. 23); bookbinding and printing were not generally separate crafts in the Colonies until about 1663. Wroth says the earliest bookbinder whose work is extant is John Ratcliff (the 3d edition of the Bay Psalm Book, 1651).

1637 The Star Chamber Decree under Charles II, this year, is claimed as a forerunner to the English copyright law (Putnam p. 18).

1638 The first college library to be established in the Colonies is at Harvard College this year (AmLA 1958, p. 143). It is a gift from John Harvard. The most influential precursor of the academic library is probably at the Sorbonne, a gift from Robert de Sorbon in 1274, formally opened in 1289; English academic libraries seem to begin at Oxford, where the nucleus for a library exists by the end of the twelfth century, cf. Thompson, pp. 255-256; 390. As service from the monastic libraries ceased, the academic libraries take over; in turn their service gives way to the Social Library Movement and the Public Library Movement.

1638 The first printing press in the Colonies is the Daye Press at Harvard College (Glaister p. 99); the press left England under Jose Glover, who died en route, and was managed by the Stephen Daye family for Glover's widow. It was at all times a private enterprise operating within the college precincts. Daye's son may have been the first printer; the first native printer was James Printer, an Indian apprentice to Samuel Green at Cambridge; the first native-born white printer was John Foster of Boston, cf. Oswald. The first press built in the Colonies is reportedly the Sauer Press of 1750, cf. Wroth, p. 82.

1639 The first printed work from the Daye Press at Harvard is accepted to be Oath of a Freeman, although no copy is extant (Steinberg p. 47). The second piece is reportedly the Peirce Almanack for the Year 1639, cf. Wroth, p. 16; the first book was the Bay Psalm Book, 1640.

1639   The term incunabula is reportedly first used to
mean the "first printed books" (Steinberg p. 19); Bernard von Mallenckrodt, in preparing a tract for the cel-
ebration (1640) by German cities of the 200th anniversary of printing, used the term in connection with books
of the period celebrated.   In 1643 and 1653, incunabula
lists appear in catalogs of libraries holding these early
imprints.

1640   The first true book to be printed in the Colonies
is accepted to be The Whole Booke of Psalmes, faith-
fully translated into English Metre, the celebrated Bay
Psalm Book (Glaister p. 99).   It is the first book printed north of Mexico, printing having reached there around
1539, cf. Carter p. 250; McMurtrie, p. 390.

1642   The invention of mezzotint for picture illustration
is ascribed to Ludwig von Seegen in this year (Glaister
p. 256).   See also 1518; 1865.

1643   The first known printed list of incunabula appears
in the Johann Saubert Historia bibliotheca republicae
Naribergensis (Besterman p. 36).

1643   Censorship: an ordinance is imposed by Parliament upon printers and booksellers this year, which af-
fects also the Colonies (Steinberg p. 191).

1643   The Naudé classification system is issued this
year (Thornton p. 169).

1644   John Milton publishes his Areopagitica this year
(Mulgan p. 57).   It is forever connected with the history
of censorship.

1647   The earliest known bookseller and "sometime publisher," exporter and importer for the Colonies, is
reported to be Hezekiah Usher, at Boston (Boynton p.
32).

1650   John Durie, The Reformed Librarie-Keeper is
published (Wormald p. 11).   Durie, or Dury, as deputy
for the Royal Library (Eng.) advanced the theory that

the librarian must not only care for the books, but show special learning and accomplishment in order to elevate the ill-paid and under-rated work. He speaks of such aspects as yearly supplements to the catalog, selective cataloging, dealing with unwanted gifts! Cf. Strout; Predeek.

1653   The Phillippe Labbé Bibliotheca nova manuscriptorum includes the incunabula in the Royal Library, Paris (Haebler p. 7), one of the earliest associations of that word with the "first printed books."

1654   The earliest reported library inventory in a U.S. college, perhaps in any U.S. library, is made at Harvard this year, by the President and Fellows (Shores p. 180).

1657   The Boston Town House is built, a booksellers' exchange like the St. Paul's center in London (Boynton p. 35).

1657   A town library is established at the Boston Town House, the bequest of Capt. Keayne (Shera pp. 19-21).

1661   John Evelyn translates the Avis of Naudé (Wormald p. 11), under the title Instructions Concerning Erecting of a Library, see also Besterman.   Also 1627.

1661   The German national library, the Deutsche Staats bibliothek at Berlin, begins this year (Esdaile p. 98).

1663   The earliest reported periodical stressing learning rather than news begins publication, the Monatsgesprache in Germany (Steinberg p. 175); periodicals as serial publications for current knowledge begin in the seventeenth century.   The only known periodical of the Classical period was the Acta, an official gazette instituted by Julius Caesar in 59 B.C., cf. *Irwin.

1663   In the American Colonies the first complete Bible is printed, John Eliot's edition in the Algonquin dialect (the New Testament was completed in 1661); in 1743 the Sauer German Bible is printed (the first German book

comes from the Sauer Press in 1739); in 1782 Robert
Aitken publishes the first complete Bible in the English
language for the Colonies.   Cf. Glaister, p. 3; Kull,
under date.

1665   The first learned periodical in England is the
Philosophical Transactions, which begins publication this
year (Steinberg p. 175).

1667   The earliest reported college librarian in the U.S.
is appointed to the Harvard College Library this year
(AmLA 1958, p. 143), Solomon Stoddard of Boston, cf.
Shores, p. 141.

1667   The first known set of library regulations in a
U.S. college is issued at Harvard, under librarian Stoddard (Shores p. 142).   See also 1700.   The Library at
Oxford had rules drawn up as early as 1367, cf. Thompson, pp. 390-391.   The earliest library regulation on
record is this, from an Athens library in the time of
Trajan (98-117):   "No book shall be taken out, since we
have sworn an oath to that effect.   It will be open from
the first hour until the sixth"--LibQ v. 7, p. 437.   As
late as 1825 a regulation of the University of Virginia
Library states that "no student shall ever be in the Library but in the presence of the Librarian, or some
Professor whom he attends."   Irwin says that the familiar notice for silence in libraries is a modern invention;
however, he quotes the well-known inscription from
Bishop Isidore's sixth-century library in Seville: "Lo-
quacity the studious writer shocks, And so be gone from
here, Sir Chatterbox," cf. Irwin, pp. 94-95.

1668   The first of the "Term Catalogues" appears under
title Mercurius Librarius; a Catalogue of Books Printed
and Published in Michaelmas Term, 1668 (McKerrow p.
138); this work was done by John Starkey until a rival
work began, by the Booksellers of London, in 1670; this
latter work continued until 1709.

1674   Thomas Hyde produces a third printed catalog for
the Bodleian, using the author's surname as the main
entry; the Hyde rules for cataloging (also known as the

Bodleian "rules for entry") also appear this year, and are widely influential in the Colonies (Ranz p. 3). See also Tuaber, p. 133.

1674   Chief Justice Sewell reports that a flogging (disciplinary) is observed with great solemnity and prayer in the library of Harvard College this year (Shores p. 213). Present-day concern with the misuse of library reading rooms has a long background; dinners and commencement gatherings were frequently scheduled at the Harvard Library, Yale Library was used for a courtroom in 1733 to try student complaints against the food furnished, and Congress is reported to have met in the College of New Jersey (Princeton) reading room.   Cf. Shores.

1674   The Oxford University Press under John Fell makes the first efforts in England toward reforms in the art of printing (Steinberg p. 143).

1674   The first release from restricted printing in the Colonies is evidenced in Marmaduke Johnson's permission to move from Cambridge to Boston to set up a press (Boynton p. 31).

1676   The earliest reported book auction in England is that by William Cooper at Little Britain, to sell the library of Dr. Lazarus Seaman (Glaister p. 37).   Estienne sets this date at 1679.

1677   The earliest reported cartography done in the Colonies is in the Hubbard Narrative of the Troubles with Indians in New England printed at Boston (Wroth p. 18); the illustrations are done by John Foster, reported to be the first engraver in the Colonies; Foster took over the Johnson press at Boston in 1675.   See also 1702.

1677   The above book is also reported to be the first illustrated book printed in the Colonies (Lehmann p. 90).

1678   The first serial publication on the installment

basis is reported to be the Moxon Mechanick Exercises
(Steinberg p. 151), although Henry Care had brought out
a "number" book, Poor Robin's Memoirs, in 1677 and
his Weekly Pacquet of Advise later that same year.

1679   A forerunner of the classed catalog with an author index is issued as the Catalogus bibliothecae Thu-
anae of the library of Jacques de Thou (Pettee p. 24).

1681   Leibnitz takes charge of the library at Wolfenbüttel, Germany, and becomes the first scholar-librarian,
interested in an organized, comprehensive, scholarly
reference library (EB ed. 11, v. 16, p. 550).

1686   The Teissier Catalogus, the earliest reported bibliography of bibliography, is published at Geneva (*Besterman v. 1, p. ix); a supplement is issued in 1705.

1688   The Cornelius à Beughem Incunabula typographiae,
the first attempt at a comprehensive bibliography of incunabula, is published at Amsterdam (Besterman p. 36).

1689   The first news sheet, forerunner of the U.S.
newspaper, appears in Boston under title New-English
Affairs, published by Samuel Green (Brigham p. 102).
The Public Occurrences appears in Boston in 1690.

1690   The first reported paper mill in the Colonies is
that of Rittenhouse and Bradford on Wissahickon Creek,
now Fairmont Park, Philadelphia (Sutermeister p. 12).
Paper-making is reported to have reached Mexico in
1575, cf. Carter, p. 250.

1690   This is the probable date for the invention of the
Dutch devised Hollander, which revolutionized the paper-
making industry (Wroth p. 124).

1691   The first "general periodical" in England appears
under title The Athenian Mercury this year (Steinberg
p. 176).   Popular tradition has it that the word magazine comes from the Arabic makhazin, meaning a storage place, and that in 1731 the Gentleman's Magazine
described itself as "A Monthly Collection to treasure

up, as in a Magazine, " the first periodical to use the term for a serial publication.

1693   The Wm. and Mary College Library probably dates from this year; Shores says it is certain that the library was a part of the founding of the College as per the original Charter, cf. Shores, p. 18.

1694   A herald of our modern duplicate exchange programs lies in the program of the Bibliothèque Nationale with England and Germany which begins this year (Tauber p. 91). In 1836, Edward Edwards proposes use of British Museum duplicates for founding a public lending library in London.

1695   The Licensing Law is abolished in England, allowing greater freedom of the press (Steinberg p. 193).

1696   The first victory for freedom of the press in the Colonies takes place in the trial of Thomas Maule, in Massachusetts Bay Colony (Wroth p. 176). Maule was arrested and tried for publishing the Truth held forth, but was acquitted. See also Lehmann.

1697   Frederick Rostgaard publishes his cataloging code, described now as quite modern in parts (Strout p. 16); in this same year Wanley raises these pertinent questions at the Bodleian: alphabetical or classified? titles and dates in language of the work? size stated? author and title annals? name of the publisher stated? editions noted? how treat "rare" books?

1698   A "free public" library is reported to open at Charleston, S.C. this year, described as the first such in the Colonies   (AmLA 1960, p. 178).

1698   A Bray Library, one made possible by the Rev. Dr. Thomas Bray of England, is reported at Trinity Parish, New York City, this year (Bostwick pp. 5-6). See also Shera, pp. 26-27. Dr. Bray became a Commissioner of the Anglican Church to Maryland in 1696; a number of Colonial parish libraries were established from his efforts. See also 1701.

1699   James Kirkwood's proposed "paroch" libraries,
in Scotland, are reported as the first attempts at county library service (Thornton p. 43).

1700's

1700   The first reported Colonial library law is passed
at Charleston, S. C., providing for administration,
management, and regulations including loans and fines
(Shera p. 28, note 36); results of a Bray gift.   See
also 1667 under regulations.

1700   Within this century "alphabetic arrangement"
comes into general use; although it reaches back at
least a thousand years (from 1964) it has not yet been
universally accepted, cf. Collison.

1701   The Yale College Library is reported to open this
year (EB ed. 11, v. 16, p. 563).   The Yale Library
was assured by the Trustees in the founding of the College, cf. Shores, pp. 20-23.

1701   The Society for the Propagation of the Gospel in
Foreign Parts (SPG) begins in England (Shera p. 28).
This is the Rev. Dr. Bray's group, which distributed
book collections throughout the Colonies.   In 1730 the
Associates of the Late Rev. Dr. Bray was formed and
still exists at Holy Trinity Church, London.

1702   The earliest known copperplate engraved illustration printed in the Colonies is ascribed to T. Emmes'
portrait of Increase Mather in the edition of Ichabod
printed by Timothy Green at Boston this year (Free
Lib. Phil. p. 46).   Certain issues of paper money had
been so engraved prior to this date; this medium is
firmly established with the coming of Francis Dewing,
about 1716, cf. Lehmann, p. 90.   A single engraved
print of Richard Mather by John Foster of Boston is
reported as early as 1670, cf. Brigham.   Boynton says
that Foster became the first engraver in the Colonies,
cf. Boynton, pp. 38-39.

1706   The prototype for the circular plan in library

architecture is the Wolfenbüttel Library, Germany, which used it without the separate book-stacks (EB 1950, v. 14, p. 26).

1709   The first English copyright law, Act 8 Anne, is enacted to protect authors from illicit printing of their works   (Glaister p. 87); it goes into effect April 1, 1710.   Hogarth is reported to have secured safeguard copyright on artists' designs in 1735, cf. Hofer, p. iv. The French copyright law is reported as of 1793.

1710   A forerunner of the Social Library is the Gentlemen's Society, founded at Spalding, England this year, and which assessed its members to form a members' library (Shera p. 55).   Thompson reports that an inscription was found, dating 200-175 B.C., presumably from the island of Cos, which shows how well-to-do citizens subscribed to a library, erected a building and contributed to a book fund, cf. *Thompson, p. 24, surely a forebear of the Social Library.

1710   The first Colonial interest in adult education is attributed to Mather's Essays to do Good (Grattan p. 15); Grattan says that the work has special significance as certainly one of the first works bearing upon adult education published in the U.S., and that Mather's proposed plan was a forerunner of all future discussion groups outside the formal classroom.

1711   J.C. Le Blon first experiments with color printing, three-color processes (Glaister p. 79).   Modern color printing developed after color photography; W. Kurtz achieved three-color process illustration in 1893, cf. McGraw, v. 10, p. 605.

1712   The pamphlet size is limited to two octavo sheets or 32 pages by Act of the English Parliament (Glaister p. 294).   To the librarian, the pamphlet is a nuisance, both in housing and statistics; he would not appreciate Orwell's reported backward look to the days of pamphleteering and his hope for a return to this format! But the war of the pamphlet size goes on.   See also 1958. There is a popular belief that the first pamphlet was an anonymous Latin love poem of the thirteenth century; Pamphilus was in the title and gradually grew into the term pamphlet, meaning a brief publication!

1713   The John Sharpe gift of 124 volumes for a "public" library is reported to have been made this year (EA 1953, v. 17, p. 350). Thornton and EB ed. 11 set the date at 1700, and as a beginning of the New York Society Library.

1714   The earliest patent on a typewriter is reported to be that of Henry Mill, in England (+Hunter p. 331). See also 1877; 1903.

1717   The earliest reported book auction in the Colonies is that of Ebenezer Pembaton at Boston (Glaister p. 37).

1718   The earliest reported use of two-color printing in the Colonies (Free Lib. Phil. p. 26); A. Bradford at Philadelphia in his Letters to His Majesty's Justices.

1719   The earliest known proposal for making paper from wood is ascribed to Raumer in his treatise to the French Royal Academy describing the American (Canada) wasp (Wroth p. 150).

1719   The Mattaire catalog of incunabula appears in his Annales typographica, issued in five volumes 1719-1741 (Glaister p. 150).

1723   The first printed library catalog in the Colonies is Harvard's Catalogus librorum bibliothecae collegii Harvardini quod est Cantabrigiae in Nova Anglia, issued this year (Pettee p. 29).   This is prepared by librarian Joshua Gee; a supplement is issued in 1725, and two other catalogs in 1773 and 1790; a catalog in manuscript existed in the first book of Harvard College Records, listing John Harvard's gifts and other bequests, cf. Shores, pp. 171-173.   See also Ranz.

1724   The earliest known periodical in the Colonies is reported to be Keimer's at Philadelphia (Wroth p. 236);

a reprint edition of the English The Independent Whig. Bradford's American Magazine and Franklin's General Magazine both appear in 1741; authorities assign the idea to Franklin.

1724 The Boston booksellers' trade association is reported established this year (Shera p. 47). Putnam reports that the first trade association in Europe was the Guild of Printers and Book-sellers of Venice, in 1548, (cf. +Putnam v. 2, p. 365), unless we accept Theodore Birt's conclusion that the leading "publishers" of Rome had organized an association by the beginning of the second century, cf. *Putnam, p. 242. See also 1st century.

1725 A prototype of type plates, the stereotype, appears in the work of William Ged, Scotland (McKerrow p. 72); earliest recorded work with solid-page type; McKerrow says, in effect, that Ged soldered the feet of type together and printed from "plates," printed two Prayer Books and an edition of Sallust; the type founders and printers strongly opposed his work and by 1739 the process was considered a failure. See also 1781; 1800. John Carter reports in The Library in 1963 that there is evidence of "soldered plates" earlier than the 1720's, cf. Library, ser. 5, v. 18, no. 4, p. 308.

1726 Allan Ramsay's lending (rental, circulating) library opens at Edinburgh (Steinberg p. 184). Altick and Thornton set the date as early as 1725. Shera says Francis Kirkman had a circulating library around 1674, in London; one is reported in Dunfermline, Scotland in 1711, and two others in London by 1720, cf. Shera, pp. 130-131.

1730 The Millington gift to New York City for a "public" library is received through the SPG; it later became part of the New York Society Library (EA 1957, v. 17, p. 356).

1731 The first recognized subscription library in the U.S. is the Library Company of Philadelphia (AmLA 1958, p. 143). It was an outgrowth of Franklin's Junto

Debating Society begun in 1727; it was chartered in 1742, had its own building 1790-1880, now is part of the Free Library of Philadelphia.

1731 A further interest in adult education (see also 1710) is shown in the Colonies through "Franklin's Library"; the Junto had as its main purpose that of continuing education, and proposed the use of a library as an essential adjunct, cf. Grattan, p. 18.

1732 The earliest reported paid librarian for a public, i.e. Social Library, is recorded as Louis Timothee, employed November 14 by the Library Company of Philadelphia (AmLA 1961, p. 178). This was Lewis Timothy, journeyman to Benjamin Franklin, sent to Charleston, S.C. in 1734 to take over the Press after Whitemarsh's death, cf. Free Lib. Phil., p. 34.

1733 The Library Company of Philadelphia publishes its first catalog (Ranz p. 15); subsequent ones were published, for promotional purposes, in 1735, 1741, 1757, 1764 and 1770; no copies extant of the 1733 or 1735 issues. See also 1741.

1733 The Book-Company of Durham, Conn. is established (Shera p. 32); a part of the Social Library Movement in the Colonies.

1734 Proceeds of a penny per gallon tax on imported liquors are voted to a U.S. college, provided a part is spent on books (Shores p. 19); the Virginia General Assembly voted such to Wm. and Mary College; private donations made up the biggest portion of the early library "funds," however, a lottery was occasionally resorted to, a college even sponsoring its own; sometimes special fees were charged students and even trustees, cf. Shores, p. 230.

1735 A further step in freedom of the press in the Colonies is expressed in the trial of John Peter Zenger, New York (Wroth p. 176); a freedom to criticize in print the conduct of public men. In 1941 a fund was raised by newspapermen to create a memorial to Zeng-

er in St. Paul's Church, East Chester, N.Y., cf. AA
1942, p. 398.

1737   Pierre Fournier devises the point system as a
unit of measure for type (Glaister p. 321).   A standard
measurement of type bodies was proposed as early as
1733 in France; Didot is reported to have improved the
Fournier system, and George Buell to have done the
earliest work on an American system in the early nineteenth century; the U.S. point system is established in
1886, cf. Updike, v. 1, pp. 28-32.

1737   "The public" becomes the patron of the author;
Steinberg says that in this year Henry Fielding dedicated his Historical Register to the public at large, making
a change from "the great" to "the multitude" as patron,
and asserting the right of the public to free access to
the printed word, cf. Steinberg, p. 153.

1737   The Barcia Epitome is published (Bühler p. 96);
an early North American sectional bibliography still in
use.

1737   A Social Library is established as a joint project
of four Connecticut towns: Guilford, Saybrook, Killing-
worth, Lyme (Shera p. 33).   This is one form of "public" library as a result of the Social Library Movement
in the U.S.

1738   Christopher Sauer I establishes his press at Germantown, Pennsylvania (Glaister p. 366).

1739   The Philogrammatican Library Company, a social
library, is founded at Lebanon, Conn. by contract with
an individual, the Rev. Solomon Williams (Shera p. 33);
this same year sees the formation of the United English
Library for the Propagation of Christian and Useful
Knowledge at Pomfret, Conn., indicating the religious
influence in the Social Library Movement.

1741   The Catalogue of Books Belonging to the Library
Company of Philadelphia is issued (Pettee p. 29).   It is
in printed form, arranged by size or format.   See

70

also 1733.

1742   The Library Company of Philadelphia is incorporated this year (Shera p. 59, note 17).   This may be
the first act of library incorporation in the Colonies.
See also 1747.

1743   The earliest reported classified subject catalog in
the U.S. is one printed by Yale this year (Pettee p. 29);
it forms a supplement to an inventory list arranged by
location, and an alphabetical author list.   It was Yale's
first printed catalog and was prepared to aid the patron
rather than to attract gifts; in 1755 a reprint was issued; in 1760 the Loganian Library, Philadelphia, used
this classified arrangement, cf. Ranz, passim.   AmLA
reports that Harvard had a subject catalog as early as
1667, cf. AmLA 1958, p. 143.

1743   The American Philosophical Society Library opens
in Philadelphia (EA 1957, v. 17, p. 356).

1744   The earliest reported auction room opens in England, that of Samuel Baker of Covent Garden; it became
eventually Sotheby and Company (Glaister p. 37).

1746   The Princeton University Library begins this year
in the College of New Jersey (EB ed. 11, v. 16, p.
563).   Shores states that the College of New Jersey had
a library (books) as soon as the College began to func-
tion--however a bookcase was not ordered until 1750,
cf. Shores, p. 28.

1747   Abraham Redwood presents funds to the Literary
and Philosophical Society of Newport, R.I., for the Redwood Library (EA 1953, v. 17, p. 351).

1747   The Redwood Library Company is incorporated
(Shera p. 59); receives the rights of corporation as "a
body politic and corporate to subsist at all times for
ever hereafter in deed and name"; becomes the prototype for succeeding similar library corporations.   See
also 1742.

1747 The National Library of Poland at Warsaw begins at this date (Esdaile p. 280).

1748 A subscription library, the Charleston Library Society, is founded in Charleston, S. C. (EA 1957, v. 17, p. 356). It began as a literary group collecting pamphlets and magazines from Britain.

1749 The University of Pennsylvania Library is established in the Charter for the "Publick" Academy at Philadelphia (Shores p. 37); the collection actually began in 1739 with a charity school for the poor; the Charter for the College is granted in 1755; in 1786 a library catalog, in two copies, is ordered prepared, cf. Shores, p. 180.

1749 The Joseph Ames Typographical Antiquities is published (Glaister p. 241); a listing of pre-seventeenth-century English printed books. Ames abandons the long "s" in this work.

1750 The building for the Redwood Library is erected at Newport, R. I. ; designed by Peter Harrison, architect, it is the oldest library building in continuous use in the U. S. (Shera p. 38).

1750 Movable type for printing music is reported to be produced by Johann Breitkopf, printer, publisher and musician, this year at Leipzig (*Hunter pp. 96-97). Spielmann says that setting and printing of music type was used by Hautain as early as 1525, and that the problem progressively eased through engraving, stereotyping, lithography, and photolithography (Spielmann p. xiii).

1750 Marbled paper appears in the Colonies this year, and cloth-backed paper for maps first appears in European countries (+Hunter p. 332).

1753 The Library Company of Providence, R. I. , is subscribed (Shera p. 117); 1500 British pounds are subscribed and a librarian is put in charge of 583 books, which are entered in a Register; in spite of a fire in

1758, it becomes the Providence Athenaeum.

1754 The New York Society Library is reported to have been established this year (EB ed. 11, v. 16, p. 563); the library of the old Knickerbocker families, which claims to have been founded by George III and to have begun as a "public" library. It has been a very influential library in U.S. history.

1754 In the same year that the King's College (Columbia) charter is granted, a collection of books is given to begin its library; a Keeper and a catalog were not provided until 1763 (Shores pp. 32-33).

1754 Earliest known report of an inter-library loan in U.S. colleges, a request from Pres. Clapp of Yale to Harvard College; loan granted (Shores p. 212).

1757 The first English wove paper appears (Clapperton p. 17); the Whatman paper used by Baskerville in an edition of Virgil. Wove paper was known in China at a much earlier date; Isaiah Thomas is reported to have used it first in the U.S., in 1795, cf. +Hunter.

1758 The New York Society Library publishes its first catalog, one of the four Colonial Social Libraries to do so (Ranz p. 15); it published two others in 1761 and 1773.

1758 Two Social Libraries, the Prince Library and the New England Library, are established at Boston by private gifts from the Rev. Thomas Prince (Shera p. 52).

1759 The British Museum opens at Montague House on January 15, formed from the Sloane, Cotton and Harley Collections (Predeek p. 29). The B.M. was established in 1753.

1760 The College of New Jersey (Princeton) publishes its first catalog (Ranz p. 15); one of the three academic catalogs published in the Colonial period.

1762 William Rind opens a circulating library at Annapolis (Shera p. 131); James Parker attempted one in New York in 1745; John Mein opened one in Boston in 1765. A rental library at Harvard, for students' convenience in required readings, is reported in the 1784 minutes of an official meeting, cf. Shores, p. 215. See also 1402.

1763 The hospital library at the Pennsylvania Hospital, Philadelphia, established this year, is credited with being the first medical library in the U.S. (Drury p. 447). An early medical library is reported at the College of Physicians, Philadelphia, in 1789, cf. Johnson, p. 369; and the New York Hospital in 1796, cf. EA 1957, v. 17, p. 356. These may have been unorganized collections rather than libraries, see also 1816.

1764 The Redwood Library of Newport, R.I., issues its first printed catalog (Ranz p. 15).

1764 The Harvard College Library is totally destroyed by fire (Brigham p. 24); in 1682 Sir John Maynard had given eight chests of books to the College; duplicates in the collection were obtained by Cotton Mather and thus escaped this disastrous fire.

1765 A censorship of student reading is recorded at Harvard in this year (Shores p. 215).

1765 The Catalogue of Mein's Circulating Library, Boston, is issued; a collection of over 650 titles, it sold for one shilling and advertised books "which are lent to read, at one pound, eight shillings, lawful money, per year; eighteen shillings per half year; or ten and eight pence per quarter; by John Mein at the London Bookstore." Cf. Shera, p. 261. See also 1762.

1765 Earliest known examples of paper title-labels appear this year (*Carter p. 123); they were printed, sometimes engraved, and applied to the paper spines of books; they continued in use until after 1832, when titling and decoration became applicable directly onto bookcloth; they were revived in the 1890's and again in the 1920's, as publishers' "gimmicks." Not to be confused with "label-title, " see 1463.

1767   The College in Rhode Island (Brown) begins the collection of books for its library (Shores p. 40); it takes the name Brown from the Treasurer of the College who, with his family, has made generous contributions to the library.   See also 1904.

1768   The first edition of the Encyclopaedia Britannica begins publication (Glaister p. 22); completed in 1771. The scholarly Chambers Encyclopaedia begins in 1859.

1768   The first "India paper" appears in England, a soft absorbent cream or buff product, imported from China (Glaister p. 189).   In 1875 an imitation of oriental papers was made for the Oxford University Press, cf. *Carter.

1769   The library of the Linonia Society, Yale, is formed (Shores p. 224).   Student libraries like these served to extend the painfully restricted use of Colonial academic libraries; one of the most outstanding was the Brothers in Unity at Yale (see items under 1846, 1848, 1851).   "Of the colleges in existence in 1830, fully 80 percent had society libraries, half of which were larger than the college libraries, "--Ranz, p. 19.   In 1784 King's College (Columbia) appointed the librarian of the student society library to be Librarian of the College, cf. Shores, p. 36.

1769   The Dartmouth College Library begins when the College is chartered this year; the collection had been in process for seven years (Shores pp. 45-46).

1769   The first "Grangerized" work is published; James Granger begins his Biographical History of England, in five volumes, completed in 1774 (Glaister p. 158).

1769   Roman face type is cut and cast in the Colonies by Abel Buell, in Connecticut (Glaister p. 367); roman face is not generally used here until 1781.   Oswald says Buell had the first type foundry in the Colonies this year; in 1772 C. Sauer II and Justus Fox established a type foundry at Germantown for their own use; in 1773 Jacob Bay set up a foundry for business with printers, cf. Oswald, p. 33. The first press is built in the Colonies this year by Isaac Doolittle, New Haven, cf. Wroth, p. 83.

1770   The Charleston Library Society publishes its first catalog, one of four Colonial Social Libraries to do so (Ranz p. 15).

1774   The first official document of the U. S. government is held to be the publication Association, printed by William and Thomas Bradford, 120 copies in a quarto of twelve pages, on October 20 (Powell p. 37); on September 22 a broadside appeared but was only an extract from the minutes; on October 24 "Extracts from the Votes and Proceedings" appears; on October 27 a Journal of the Proceedings (not to be confused with a later serial) is printed.

1775   The earliest reported completely American book is published (Wroth p. 106); The Impenetrable Secret has its paper, ink, printing and publishing all made or done in the Colonies; no copy extant; it was advertised in the Pennsylvania Mercury of June 23, 1775.

1775   Thomas Bewick develops wood-engraving and makes it popular for book illustration (Glaister p. 442); he does his best work this year, see also Bland, p. 224.

1776   Adam Smith first describes the principle of division of labor in his Wealth of Nations (Hawley p. 1). Although some cognizance is taken by libraries of the principle, apparently nothing constructive administratively is done until 1923, which see.

1777   The first Federal library in the U. S. is credited to be the Army Library, West Point, established this year (AmLA 1960, p. 178). The library for the West Point Military Academy opened in 1812, cf. Johnson, p. 356.

1780   The American Academy of Arts and Sciences Library is founded (EA 1957, v. 17, p. 356a). The founding of scholarly society libraries, which contributed so much to Colonial library service, continued into the next century, but the Social Library Movement relieved them of their "public" service: 1812, The Academy of Natural Sciences, Philadelphia; 1818, New York Academy of Sciences; 1829, Massachusetts Horticultural Society; 1831, Boston Society of Natural History.

1780   The earliest known use of a control card for information storage is by Jacquard with his control cards for looms (Casey p. 3). Such a loom may be seen in all its glory, cards flying at control, in the Deutsches Museum, Munich.

1780   Steel writing pens replace the quill (+Hunter p. 339). Lamb says that about 190 B. C., as parchment displaced papyrus, and with the later establishment of the Roman formal capital letters, the quill pen began to displace the reed; as early as 150 B. C. the Romans made pens of metal, cf. Lamb, passim.

1780   A duplication process by a press-copying machine (using a glutinous ink and moistened sheets of thin paper) is reported this year, an invention of James Watt; first used by the Federal Government in 1790 to produce copies of outgoing documents in the Department of State; went out of use only in 1912, with the introduction of carbons on a typewriter, cf. *Schellenberg, p. 82.

1781   A forerunner of the modern reserve book system is seen in the proposal submitted to the officers of Harvard College by Prof. Wigglesworth to "reserve" weekly selections of titles from the College Library, cf. Shores, pp. 216-217.

1781   The second invention of type-plates (see also 1725), the forerunner of stereotype, occurs this year (McKerrow p. 72); the idea is again abandoned. Glaister sets the date at 1784, by Foulis and Tilloch at Glasgow.

1783   The Social Friends Library is founded at Dart-

mouth College, one of the early student society libraries (Shores p. 225); it combined with the United Fraternity Library in 1790; at its dissolution in 1799 the
joint library had 1,000 volumes; later each organization
separately developed a library of equal size. See also
1769; 1798.

1783   The first copyright laws in the U.S. were state
laws; Connecticut reportedly passes the first such this
year (Nicholson p. 5).

1785   The first known architectural designs for the library and its public are by Boulée (EB 1950, v. 14, p.
26), in his Memoir, with its plans for tiers for books.
The most intriguing library building situation is Chicago's use of the old water reservoir for its library after
the great fire in 1871; the most delightful situation is
the decision in 1965 to preserve the Jefferson Market
Courthouse in New York's Greenwich Village by using
it as a branch library.

1785   The earliest reported U.S. directory, one for the
city of Philadelphia, appears this year (Brigham p. 53).

1785   The first publishing house in the U.S. opens at
Philadelphia under Mathew Carey (Lehmann p. 126).
See also 1472.

1786   The British government printing office is established, His Majesty's Stationery Office (HMSO) (Steinberg p. 222).

1786   The United Fraternity Library, a student social
library, is founded at Dartmouth College (Shores p. 225).
See also 1783.

1787   The first printed catalog of the British Museum
is begun (Thornton p. 182).

1787   The long "S" is reported to be officially abandoned this year (Mann p. 39), although it continues to
appear in print.   Glaister says the earliest known aban-
donment was by Ames in 1749; Steinberg says Bell aban-

doned it in his edition of Shakespeare in 1785. See also McKerrow, p. 309. Updike says lower case "i" and "j" were first differentiated in Spain in the late 1500's; Elzevir is supposed to have differentiated lower case "u" and "v," "i" and "j," at Leyden sometime before 1616; in England the lower case "u" and "j" became general practice about 1630, and about 1700, with upper and lower case, the "u" became the vowel, the "v" the consonant, cf. Updike, v. 1, pp. 22-23.

1789 A classed catalog with an alphabetical author index is issued by the Library Company of Philadelphia (Pettee p. 29). This is an early influential use of this arrangement (see also 1679); in 1815, LC uses it; in 1824, the American Philosophical Society Library; in 1826, the Charleston Library Society; in 1837, the New York Mercantile Library, cf. Ranz, pp. 26; 56.

1789 The first proposal for a library for the U.S. Congress is made to the Congress on August 6 by Elbridge Gerry: "report a catalog of books . . . estimate of expense . . . best mode of procuring . . ." (Mearns p. 1); the first official proposal came June 23, 1790, to appropriate a thousand dollars, with five hundred annually, to purchase books for a "public library," in the sense of a Social Library.

1789 The first printed document of the new U.S. Congress appears (Brigham p. 130); it listed the first acts passed at the first session of the first Congress.

1789 A Federal library: Department of State under Jefferson, the first Secretary of State (EA 1957, v. 17, p. 357i).

1790 The Federal Copyright Law in the U.S. is ratified (Rogers p. 4). Major changes were made in 1906 and contemplated in 1965; interesting parallels have been shown: 1906 legislative hearing called on Wednesday, June 6, with testimony from the Librarian of Congress (Putnam), R.R. Bowker, Victor Herbert, John Phillips Sousa; 1965 hearing called on Wednesday, June 26, with testimony from the Librarian of Congress

(Mumford), John Hersey, Rex Stout, Herman Wouk and
E. Janeway, cf. LCIB, v. 24.

1790   The Archives Nationales of Paris is opened, the
first reported official national archives institution
(*Schellenberg p. 4); the National Assembly established
the archival institution in 1789.   The origin of archival
collections disappears into antiquity; the Egyptians had
such collections, as did Assurbanipal in Mesopotamia of
the 600's B.C. , and the Athenians in the temple to Me-
troon in the fifth and fourth centuries B.C. ; the Romans
kept extensive public records and are credited with beginning the "registry system" in their commentarii
diurni (daily court journals); archival activities continued even during the Middle Ages; sixteenth-century
Spain and seventeenth-century Austria are reported to
have had outstanding collections.   In 1838 England established its central archival institution in the Public
Records Office, for historical and cultural reasons; in
1934 the U.S. established its National Archives.   Cf.
*Schellenberg, passim.

1790   A classified catalog arranged alphabetically by
class, and by author under class, is issued by Harvard;
the classes were not subdivided (Ranz pp. 25; 57); this
was an attempt at the alphabetico-classed arrangement;
in 1809 the Baltimore Library Company issued a similar one; in 1821, Bowdoin College did also.   See also
1861.

1790   The Glasgow cataloging rules are issued this year
(Dewey ed. 16, Introd.).

1790   William Nicholson works on the earliest known
mechanical press, in London (Glaister p. 329).

1791   The earliest known national cataloging code is
reported in France this year (Strout p. 17).

1791   The earliest reported use of a "card catalog" is
ascribed to France, in this year (Strout p. 17).

1791   A classed catalog with subdivision on a generous

scale is issued by Yale; a first in the practice of subdividing the various subject classes (Ranz p. 56); in 1861 a climax in this proliferation of classes and subclasses is reached in the LC published catalog with 179 sequences.

1791 The earliest reported true theological seminary library is St. Mary's in Baltimore, founded this year (Johnson p. 366); in 1794 a Protestant one is reported for the Presbyterian Seminary, Beaver County, Pennsylvania. This is not to ignore the uncountable number of "ministerial" collections in the Colonies.

1791 The Massachusetts Historical Society is founded, the only historical society in the U.S. before 1800; with the turn of the century the general interest in local and national history increased and the historical societies spread rapidly, with 65 by 1850, 223 by 1905, 1800 by 1957; in 1884 the American Historical Association was founded; preservation of archival materials was vested in these societies until the twentieth century, cf. Schellenberg, pp. 20-21.

1792 The Library Company of Philadelphia opens reference service to the public; books continue to circulate to members only (EB ed. 11, v. 16, p. 563). In 1765, at Harvard, new regulations provided for "Times specify'd when Gentlemen may consult Books in the Library [which] are not to be lent,"--Shores, p. 192. No provision for reference service was in Yale's early regulations.

1792 The Queens College (Rutgers) Library probably begins this year, with a bequest from Peter Leydt, although some books were available to the College before this (Shores pp. 44-45).

1792 The Georgetown University Library is reported to begin this year (EA 1957, v. 17, p. 356).

1793 The earliest reported catalog in the U.S. for selected books for a public library is that of Thaddeus Mason Harris, librarian at Harvard, who publishes at

Boston the Selected Catalogue . . . to Forme a Social
Library (Shera p. 110); described as the earliest attempt for a book selection policy for public libraries.
Rosenwald reports that La tabula della salute, printed
at Florence in 1494, contained the first known printed
"Recommended Reading List, " cf. Quart. J v. 22, no.
3, p. 162.

1793 A subscription library is founded for Dublin, New
Hampshire, the Union Library (EA 1957, v. 17, p. 356);
another part of the Social Library Movement in the U.S.

1793 The Williams College Library is reported to begin this year (EA 1957, v. 17, p. 356).

1794 A subscription library is founded in Boston (EA
1957, v. 17, p. 356); another part of the Social Library
Movement in the U.S.

1795 The University of North Carolina Library is reported to open this year (EA 1960, v. 17, p. 417), the
last of the eighteenth-century academic libraries in the
U.S.; with the turn of the century the Social Libraries
begin to serve the general user of libraries.

1796 The earliest reported legislation permitting the
founding of library corporations [for Social Libraries]
is enacted by New York State this year (Joeckel p. 6).

1796 The first deposit copies under the U.S. copyright
law of 1790 are received by the Department of State
(Rogers p. 12).

1796 Early work with lithography is done by Aloysius
Senefelder at Munich (Glaister p. 239). Carter speaks
of "lithographed" books as early as 992 in China, cf.
Carter p. 22.

1796 A subscription library is reported to open at Baltimore (EA 1957, v. 17, p. 356), another part of the
Social Library Movement in the U.S.

1796 Portugal's national library at Lisbon begins this

year. It assumed the name Biblioteca Nacionale in 1836 (Esdaile p. 201).

1797   John West issues what may be the first trade catalog in the U.S., A catalogue of Books Published in America and for Sale at the Bookstore of John West, printed by Samuel Etheridge, at Boston (Lehmann p. 133). May also be the first attempt at a national bibliography in the U.S., cf. Rogers, p. 97.

1798   The Philermenian Society at Brown College begins a library to augment the library services to students (Shores p. 225).

1798   Legislation to permit the founding of library corporations [for Social Libraries] is enacted by the State of Massachusetts (Joeckel p. 6). Shera says all six of the New England states freely granted private corporations the privilege to establish and manage book collections, cf. Shera, p. 183.

1798   A paper-making machine is introduced by Robert, in France (+Hunter p. 345).

1798   The national library, De Koninblijke Bibliotheek at The Hague, begins this year (Esdaile p. 154).

1799   The last of the chained libraries in England (Magdalene College) is reported to disappear this year (Thornton p. 33). Clark says unchaining of the books in England began at Eton in 1719, reached the Bodleian in 1757 and King's College, Cambridge in 1777; however, as late as 1815 some books were chained in St. Peters, Liverpool, at the request of John Fells, who gave thirty pounds for a theological library, cf. Clark, p. 263. Have we "rechained" the books in the use of locked areas, turnstiles and electric eyes?

1799   An English law, 39 George III cop. 79, requires that the name and address of the printer be placed in every work from his press (*Carter p. 116). The trying absence of imprints is proof to catalogers that this law was all too often broken.

1800   The Library of Congress is formally established, "for the use of Congress" (Mearns p. 6).

1800   The earliest reported book club is a Swiss cooperative one (Steinberg p. 239). Book clubs are not reported in England until 1939. See also 1926.

1800   A revival of the type plate is made by Wilson and Stanhope in London, a perfection of the earlier plates (McKerrow p. 72). See also 1725; 1781.

1800   Paper from straw is proposed by Matthias Koops in his Invention of Paper, London (*Hunter p. 76); the edition is published on all-straw paper.

1801   The American Company of Booksellers is organized (Growell p. iii).

1801   Dennie's The Port Folio begins publication in Philadelphia (Growoll p. xvii); an early form of trade bibliography in the U.S.

1802   The first librarian is appointed for LC by the President; he is John James Beckley, who serves part-time, being also Clerk of the House (Mearns p. 11); the Rev. George Wright, librarian of the New York Society Library, became in fact, though not in name, the first "Librarian of Congress," cf. Mearns, p. 4.

1802   The U.S. copyright law is amended to require a notice of copyright in the book itself (Nicholson p. 6).

1802   A Book Fair is held in New York City by the American Company of Booksellers (Growoll p. iii); a literary fair for the trade not the public.

1802   The first catalog for LC is prepared by format this year (Mearns p. 11); an inventory of the collection, it is placed in the quarters assigned in the new Capitol; Jefferson also prepares his famous desiderata list this year, as a future buying guide; the invoice of 1800 from

Messrs. Cadell and Davies might more properly be called the "first catalog, " cf. Mearns, passim.

1803 The Bingham gift is made to Salisbury, Conn. for a Library for Youth (Shera p. 158). Caleb Bingham gave the library for the children of Salisbury; Lucas says it opened in 1807; Bostwick calls it the first example of municipal aid to libraries (see 1810). Cf. Drury; Bostwick; Lucas; Joeckel.

1803 The Suhler Press, the first automatic platen press by König, appears (Glaister p. 373).

1803 The Federal library in the Treasury Department is reported to open this year (Johnson p. 353).

1804 The earliest reported free juvenile public library opens March 2, at New Lebanon, N. Y. , under the auspices of Juvenile Society for the Acquisition of Knowledge (AmLA 1960, p. 178). See also 1807.

1804 A catalog of the Booksellers of Boston is published, constituting an early attempt at trade and national bibliography (Rogers p. 97).

1804 The "coonskin library" of Ames, Ohio, begins (Marshall p. 48); coonskins are sent to Boston in exchange for books; it also served Marietta, Ohio. See also item on branch libraries under 1871.

1805 The first cylinder machine for making paper on a continuous roll is invented by Joseph Bramah, Pimlico (Glaister p. 94). See also 1809.

1807 An alphabetical catalog, by author, is prepared with a classified index by George Campbell for the Philadelphia Library Company (Ranz p. 26); little notice is taken of the arrangement until 1830, which see.

1807 A children's library opens at Salisbury, Conn. (Lucas p. 4). See also 1803.

1807 The Boston Athenaeum opens, probably the first

in the U.S. (Drury p. 21); it began as the Anthology Reading Room affiliated with the Monthly Anthology. The Athenaeum Movement spread rapidly and broadly throughout the U.S., cf. Shera; EB ed. 1957.

1808 The first major effort toward a complete national bibliography for the U.S. is begun by Isaiah Thomas with a catalog of titles in his History of Printing in America (Rogers p. 8); in 1874 the American Antiquarian Society published a second edition.

1809 Dickinson improves the papermaking machine, and machine-made paper begins to supplant handmade for all ordinary purposes of book production, cf. McKerrow; and Glaister. The printed book becomes cheaper, and the free public library more possible.

1809 The administration of James Madison sees the establishment of a library for the White House in Washington (Johnson p. 354). In the year 1964 a special collection was assembled, under a committee headed by the Director of the Yale Library, to be a permanent White House Library.

1810 Traveling libraries are reported in Scotland as early as this date (Bostwick p. 17).

1810 The earliest reported case of municipal funds being voted in the U.S. to aid a library occurs at Salisbury, Conn. (Shera p. 159); these were not "regular" funds. See also 1827.

1810 An Athenaeum is established at Salem, Mass. (EA 1957, v. 17, p. 356a). See also 1807.

1810 The Brunet Manual du libraire et de l'amateur de libres is published in three volumes at Paris (Glaister p. 48); a five-volume edition appears in 1860-1864. Benjamin Pierce is one of the first in the U.S. to use the Brunet classification, cf. Ranz, p. 27. See also 1830.

1811 The earliest reported patients' library opens at

the Massachusetts General Hospital, Boston; a collection of religious books (EA 1957, v. 17, p. 356r).

1811   Massachusetts enacts legislation providing for the exchange of state documents with other states (Shera p. 212); this lays the cornerstone for the State Library, established in 1826, see also 1818.

1811   The national libraries of the Scandinavian countries begin in early royal or university collections; the Universetetsbibliotsket at Oslo is founded this year; Det Kongelige Bibliotek at Copenhagen was founded in the seventeenth century; the Kungliga Biblioteket at Stockholm in the sixteenth century; the University of Helsenki Library in 1640, cf. Esdaile, pp. 207-233.

1812   The American Antiquarian Society is founded (Brigham p. 1).   Its library is formed from the private collection of Isaiah Thomas, cf. Shera, p. 209.

1812   Stereotyping is introduced into the U.S. (+Hunter p. 352).

1812   König builds his first stop-cylinder press, in Britain (Glaister p. 94); he patented the iron press in 1810.

1813   Senefelder improves lithographic printing processes by discovering a substitute for the heavy stone (Glaister p. 373); his work with metal plates began in 1805.

1813   The earliest reported stereotyped book in the U.S. is produced this year (+Hunter p. 352).

1813   The first successful ink roller becomes available to replace the ink balls used since the fifteenth century (Glaister p. 191).

1814   The earliest reported U.S. government document deposit is established, by act of Congress, at the American Antiquarian Society (Brigham p. 130).

1814   The Library of Congress is destroyed by fire

(Mearns p. 15).

1814 An Athenaeum is established at Philadelphia (EA 1957, v. 17, p. 356a). See also 1807.

1815 The Library of Congress is re-established with Jefferson's private library, purchased by Congress (Mearns p. 20); a collection of 6,487 volumes, valued at $23,950; a distinctive private library passes to the U.S. government and changes the character of LC from a "special" to a "general" library, one step closer to a national library.

1815 The Library of Congress issues a classed catalog with an index to authors (Ranz p. 26); titled Catalogue of the Library of the United States, it is for the Jefferson library, cf. Adams, p. 94, note; Pettee, p. 29.

1815 The Library of Congress gets its first full-time librarian, George Watterston (Rogers p. 14).

1816 A true medical library opens at Harvard, credited with being the first such (AmLA 1960, p. 178). See also item under 1763. In 1965 the Harvard Medical Library and the Boston Medical Library (1875) combined to form the largest university medical library in the U.S.

1816 The earliest reported legislative authority for establishment of county library systems is enacted by Indiana (Joeckel p. 14).

1816 The first experiments with curved stereos for cylinder printing are carried out by William Nicholson (Glaister p. 388).

1816 The earliest reported cylinder paper-machine made in the U.S. is brought out by Gilpin this year (Lehmann p. 87). The earliest operation of a paper-machine is reported in 1817, cf. +Hunter, p. 353.

1817 The earliest reported true law library in the U.S. is established at Harvard this year (AmLA 1960, p. 178).

There were law book collections in the U.S. before this date; Johnson reports the Philadelphia Law Association Library in 1802, and the Boston Social Law Library in 1804. The oldest English law library is reported to be that of Lincoln's Inn, London, dated 1497 (EB ed. 11, v. 16, p. 557).

1817 The itinerating libraries of Samuel Brown, Scotland, traveling subscription libraries, begin this year (EB ed. 1, v. 16, p. 564).

1817 An Athenaeum opens at Portsmouth, N.H. (EA 1957, v. 17, p. 356a). See also 1807.

1818 The earliest known Mechanics' Library in the U.S. opens at Bristol, Conn. (Shera p. 230). The line of demarcation between these and the Mercantile libraries was not sharp, but the organizations themselves were dissimilar; however, both emphasized continuing education through books, raising of moral standards, providing suitable places for young peoples' leisure hours, raising cultural standards, and both were a part of the Social Library Movement. Their beginnings were in the workers' institutes of England; in 1760 lectures were held in Glasgow for such an institute; in 1795 Birmingham established the first Artisans' Library; in 1823 Liverpool established the Mechanics' and Apprentices' Library. This movement in the U.S. spread as rapidly and broadly as the Athenaeum.

1818 The New Hampshire State Library opens under an act authorizing the secretary of state "to collect and arrange all books belonging to the State" (Shera p. 212). Shera says this is the first State Library in the U.S. There is much diversity of opinion here, which seems to stem from beginnings as social libraries at earlier times than establishment as State agencies. There is a claim for New Jersey as early as 1811, for Pennsylvania in 1813, for New York State in 1818, cf. Predeek; Thornton; EB ed. 1950. "State Library" has a peculiar meaning to U.S. libraries in that it differentiates the "national" library of the Federal government from those belonging to the several State governments.

1818   Perkins and Heath (U.S. and Britain) do serious work with processes for steel engraving (Glaister p. 385).

1818   Bowdler's expurgated edition of Shakespeare is published (Glaister p. 44). "Bowdlerize" becomes a term meaning to expurgate.

1818   The Almanach auf das Jahr, measuring 5/8 x 7/16 inches, produced by C.F. Müller, Germany, is probably the first miniature book done by lithography (Spielmann p. 4).

1820   The earliest reported Mercantile Library Association is established at Boston (Drury p. 33). See also 1818.

1820   A Mechanics' Apprentices' Library is established in Boston (Shera p. 230). Possibly one is established in New York City also, cf. EB ed. 11, v. 16, p. 563. See also 1818.

1820   Contribution to library education: Ebert, The Education of a Librarian (White p. 71).

1821   The Church Press for mechanical type-composing and printing is patented (Glaister p. 67). William Church, a native of Vermont, did his work at Birmingham, England.

1821   The Mercantile Library Association is established in Philadelphia (Thornton p. 188). See also 1818.

1822   The first permanent photograph by a camera, the work of Niepce in France, appears this year (Glaister p. 276). The camera obscura supposedly first appeared in 1000 A.D., a tent with a small hole; in 1685 it had become a box with a lens; in 1725 Johann Schulze was working with silver nitrate and light; in 1802 Thomas Wedgewood could make contact copies of leaves on glass, cf. LibT v. 5, no. 2, p. 265; Fabre.

1822   "Book cloth," a dyed and treated calico, is introduced by Pickering and Leighton this year (Glaister p. 38). This cloth, devised as a novelty, led to edition-binding, which in turn made possible cheaper yet well-bound books, cf. *Carter, pp. 160-161. See also 1832.

1824 The American Philosophical Society issues a classed catalog with an index to authors in which the first real attention, in the U.S., is given to corporate entries (Ranz p. 32).

1824 The Library of Congress receives rooms fitted and decorated for its own use (Mearns p. 32).

1824 The basic principles of engraving on metal by photography are discovered by Niepce, in France (Glaister p. 306).

1825 The earliest reported "annual" in the U.S. begins under title The Atlantic Souvenir (Brigham p. 20). This is one of the long line of sentimental collections of "keepsake" literature in vogue for some time in the U.S. and England. See also 1912. The "yearbook," as a reference tool, has borrowed something from the Almanac, the Annual, the news magazine, and the Annal.

1825 A patent is obtained for a roller to make machine-made paper look like handmade, including a watermark (+Hunter p. 355).

1826 The Charleston Library Society issues a classed catalog with alphabetical index to authors (Ranz p. 26).

1826 In this year Josiah Holbrook sets forth a scheme that becomes the American Lyceum Movement; in 1830 a model constitution recommended a library as a primary objective; the Movement died in the 1860's, but its themes reappeared in the Chautauqua Movement of the twentieth century, cf. Shera, pp. 226-227.

1827 The Governor of New York recommends that a small collection of books be placed in every school-

91

house; this is the earliest reported attempt in the U.S. at a state-supported school library (EA 1957, v. 17, p. 356x).

1827   The Horne cataloging code and classification scheme is published for Queens College, Cambridge (Strout p. 17).

1827   Castine, Maine grants regular municipal funds to produce and support a social library (Joeckel p. 15). Its objectives were to excite a fondness for books, to prevent idleness and immorality and to promote a diffusion of useful knowledge, all arguments which were to be used in later campaigns throughout the U.S. to support free public libraries, cf. Shera, p. 238. See also 1810.

1827   An Athenaeum is established at Portland, Maine (EA 1957, v. 17, p. 356s). See also 1807.

1827   The Fourdrinier paper-machine reaches the U.S. this year (+Hunter p. 356). It was first patented in 1806, cf. Glaister, p. 145.

1827   The enameled paper processes are patented in England (+Hunter p. 356).

1828   Lithography is brought to the U.S. by Barnett and Doolittle (Glaister p. 239); the first British patents were obtained in 1801; the earliest known English book with lithographic printing appears in 1803.

1828   An Athenaeum is established at Zanesville, Ohio (EA 1957, v. 17, p. 356a). See also 1807.

1828   The first Webster's dictionary is published by Noah Webster under title The American Dictionary of the English Language (Shove p. 33, note). His first work of a similar nature, the Compendious Dictionary, appeared in 1806; at his death in 1841 the Merriman Company acquired the dictionary. The first Funk and Wagnalls appears in 1893; the first Century, in twelve volumes, in 1911.

1828   The National Library of Greece at Athens opens this year (Esdaile p. 185).

1829   Louis Braille devises a form of writing for the blind reader (Glaister p. 45); in 1850 William Moon devises a form of Braille writing which is embossed rather than punched, cf. Glaister.

1829   The Mechanics' Institute Library in Cincinnati opens (EA 1957, v. 17, p. 356a).   See also 1818.

1829   The Encyclopedia Americana begins this year (Kull).   The first edition of Collier's is published in 1949.

1830   An alphabetical catalog, by authors, with a classified or "systematic index" is prepared for Harvard College by Benjamin Peirce, and received with great acclaim (Ranz p. 27).   See also 1807.

1830   The earliest known use of the title "Library of Congress" appears in the Library's general catalog for this year (Adams p. 94).

1830   The earliest reported technological library in the U.S. opens at Franklin Institute (EA 1957, v. 17, p. 357q).

1830   The earliest reported abstract journal begins as the Pharmazeutisches Zentralblatt (Casey p. 579); it is known today as the Chemisches Zentralblatt.

1830   A forerunner of the published lists of copyright deposits appears in the Patentees Manual prepared by William Elliot (Rogers p. 20); in 1820 the first listing of deposits, resulting from the operation of the U.S. copyright law, appeared in A List of Patents Granted by the United States; in 1822 Elliot prepared the first copyright deposit list for the U.S. Patent Office.

1830   The first U.S. patent for wood-pulp paper is reported as of this year (Weeks p. 225); Wooster and Holmes, patentees; some paper made and used. Hunter says it is possible some wood-pulp paper was made by Munsell at Meadeville, Pa. this year, cf. +Hunter p. 357. Glaister says that the use of wood for paper-making dates from 1843 in Germany, cf. Glaister, p. 442. Hunter says further that the first useful paper from a chemical wood process was in 1851 by Burges and Watt, who brought their process to the U.S. around 1854. From the time of the wasp in Raumer's day (see 1719), wood-pulp paper has been a troublemaker; even the reports of its development are in disagreement; the only thing of which we are sure, libraries begin to realize the disastrous effects from its use in the 1930's.

1831 Deposit copies under the U.S. copyright law of 1790 begin to be made with the District Courts, to be forwarded to the Department of State (Rogers p. 12).

1832 A law is passed to enlarge and improve a law department of LC for use of the Supreme Court (Mearns p. 39).

1832 A sewing machine for bookbinding is invented by Philip Watt (Glaister p. 245); in 1871 David Smyth patents the first thread-sewing machine for bookbinding; sometime between 1871-1879 the Brehmers develop a machine to wire-stitch books, cf. Glaister.

1832 A bindery for "edition work," casing of books instead of hand-binding, is established by Bradley in Boston (Lehmann p. 149). The cheaper casing work, adopted by the publishers, begins to replace custom hand-binding; England is reported to have its first "case bound" book this year, done by John Murray, cf. Glaister, p. 60.

1832 The first Baedeker appears, a guide to a Rhine journey from Mainz to Coblenz (Glaister p. 163). The Baedeker guide books are a continuing reference tool because of their attention to details.

1832 The forerunner of "exchange programs" (materials) is seen in Britain's plans this year to exchange materials with France (Tauber p. 91).

94

1832 The American State Papers, compiled by General William Hickey, begins publication; a compilation of government documents covering 1789-1833 was completed in 1861 (Powell p. 24).

1832 Federal library: War Department is reported to begin a library this year (Johnson p. 353); also the Coast and Geodetic Survey.

1833 Photographic processes are developed by Daguerre and the daguerrotype appears in France (Glaister p. 97). We are on our way to cheaper illustrations, text reproduction, micro-filming, "reduced printing," and other devices to improve library services.

1833 Automation begins with Babbage and his machines (Booth p. 14). In 1642 Pascal produced the adding machine, in 1671 Leibnitz worked with "multiplication," in 1786 von Müller worked with "difference," now Babbage applies the "analytical," cf. EB ed. 11, v. 4, p. 972.

1833 A Mechanics' Institute Library opens in New York City (EA 1957, v. 17, p. 356). See also 1818.

1833 The earliest reported use of the dust jacket, on Heath's Keepsake (Glaister p. 203). This heir to the book wrapper was not widely adopted until the end of the nineteenth century; in 1876 Unwin's probably used the first illustrated ones; after 1910 blurbs begin to appear on them, when the jacket becomes important to book sales; in 1923 the British Museum began its collection of them, cf. Rosner.

1833 Peterborough, N.H. votes a "public tax" as regular support for a public library (Bostwick p. 8). The money came from the State for educational purposes and was applied to a town library by the city, cf. Shera, p. 163.

1834 Lowndes' The Bibliographer's Manual of English Literature is published in four volumes (*Carter p. 129); it is revised in 1858-1864 by Henry G. Bohn.

1835   The earliest known legislation for school-district libraries in the U.S. is enacted by New York State (Bostwick p. 6); the earliest movement toward school-district libraries was in 1812, also in New York State. Although these libraries were inadequate, the laws establishing them did define a system of library service, one providing for taxation, semi-free service, state aid, and adult education, cf. Shera; Joeckel. In 1837 Massachusetts enacted such legislation and other states followed; all were permissive not mandatory; the Lowell (Mass.) City School Library became the Lowell Public in 1883.

1835   The Michigan State Constitution directly provides for libraries and their support (Joeckel p. 54); the section on education instructs the legislature to provide at least one library in each township, using proceeds from penal fines.   AmLA sets the date at 1838; EA ed. 1957 says that Indiana's original constitution (1816) also provided for libraries.

1835   Delessert designs the circular reading room for the Bibliothèque Nationale (EB 1950, v. 14, p. 26); the earliest reported separation of readers and storage.

1836   The Library of the Surgeon-General's Office is established (EA 1953, v. 17, p. 357s).   Forerunner of the U.S. National Library of Medicine.

1836   A Federal library: The Patent Office is established (EB ed. 11, v. 16, p. 562).   The Official Gazette begins publication in 1872.

1836   The Spanish national library, La Biblioteca Nacional at Madrid, begins this year (Esdaile p. 191); it evolves from a royal library of 1712.

1837   The earliest consideration of international copyright in the U.S. is shown in the Henry Clay Bill this year (Rogers p. 36).

1837   Gottfried Englemann obtains the first patents for color photography, France (Glaister p. 239).   See also 1711.

1837   The Belgian national library, La Bibliothèque Royale de Belgique at Brussels, begins this year (Esdaile p. 134).

1838   An alphabetical catalog is prepared by Oliver A. Taylor for Andover Theological Seminary; is described as having "no superior" by Jewett (Ranz p. 27); made skilled use of added entries and cross references.

1838   The Hain Repertorium Bibliographicum is completely published; it was begun in 1826 (ALA 1930, p. 53).   This is a convenient first reference for incunabula; in 1895-1902 W.A. Copenger published a supplement cited as Hain-Copenger; in 1891 K. Burger published an Indices; in 1905 D. Reichling began a series of Appendices, cf. *Carter.

1838   The Caoutchouc binding is devised by T. Hancock, using a rubber solution in place of thread (Glaister p. 57).   This is a precursor of unsewn binding.

1838   Thornton reports a case of a library being sold to pay the debts of the librarian: the Juliana Library, Lancaster, founded 1770 by Thomas Penn (Thornton p. 180).

1839   The Panizzi "91 rules," a code for rules of entry, are approved (Predeek p. 39) in England.   In 1841 they are published, cf. Ranz, p. 31.   They are a great influence on U.S. codes, cf. Strout, p. 18.

1839   Albrecht Beyer discovers the process of reflex printing, a means of reproducing a document without type (Glaister p. 343).

1839   Dancer does early work with the processes of micro-filming; though not serious it did contribute to the field of micro-photography (Doss p. 68).   See also LibT v. 5, no. 2, p. 276.

1840   The earliest recorded exchange program for LC

97

is approved by Congress; an exchange of public documents and duplicates (Mearns p. 55). As early as 1724 there was a ruling on duplicates handed down by the Corporation for Harvard College; in 1731 Yale permitted the sale of duplicates for the benefit of the Library, cf. Shores, p. 170. See also 1867.

1840   The earliest known use of a pre-punched card for information storage is that of Babbage in statistical control (Casey p. 3).

1840   The earliest reported separate building for an academic library in the U.S. is that for the University of South Carolina, Columbia (AmLA 1960, p. 178); previously reported was Harvard's building in 1841.

1840   The James Lenox Collection begins this year; now in the New York Public (Glaister p. 218).

1843   An author catalog for Brown University, with an alphabetical topical index, is prepared by Jewett (Pettee p. 32). It is influential in that it breaks the monopoly of logical arrangement in classed catalogs, and introduces an alphabetical subject arrangement which permits interfiling, cf. Ranz, pp. 57; 63.

1843   Labrouste designs the Ste. Genevieve Library, Paris, which becomes the prototype for several library buildings in the U.S. (EB 1950, v. 14, p. 26).

1843   The Mercantile Library Association is established in Bangor, Maine (EA 1957, v. 17, p. 356a). See also 1818.

1844   A catalog for the Boston Mercantile Library is issued, described as the first of the dictionary catalogs in the U.S.; the practice of entering books under author and title, in one alphabet, has reached its height (Ranz pp. 30; 63).

1844   An alphabetico-classed catalog is issued for the New York Mercantile Library (Ranz p. 29).

1844   The Fox Talbot The Pencil of Nature is published
with the first photographic book illustrations (LibT v. 5,
no. 2, p. 266).

1844   Mass production by reprints: the first proposals
for reproducing the texts of books by photography are
made (LibT v. 5, no. 2, p. 266).   A look forward to
University Microfilms in 1958.

1845   The Statutes at Large of the United States is first
published by Little, Boston, 1845-1873; in 1875 the GPO
takes over publication (Shove p. 59); after 1936 the title
changes to United States Statutes at Large.   Collected
editions of the U.S. Statutes appear as follows: Fol-
well, 1789-1814, twelve volumes; Bioren & Duane, 1789-
1843, ten volumes; Little, Brown, 1789-1873, seventeen
volumes; State Department edition by GPO, 1873 to now.

1845   A Federal library at the Naval Observatory is
reported to begin this year (Johnson p. 354); also a library for the Naval Academy, Annapolis.

1846   Deposit copy under the copyright law is to be
sent to both the Smithsonian and to LC; the latter publishes the first "lists" as a section of its printed card
holdings (Rogers p. 25); the deposit is discontinued in
1859.   See also 1865.

1846   The Smithsonian Institution and its library are established in Washington with Joseph Henry as first director (Mearns p. 99); from the bequest of James Smith-
son, made in 1838 to the United States of America for
purposes of increasing and diffusing knowledge.   Its
divisions are Bureau of Ethnology, 1879; National Museum; National Zoological Park, 1890; Astrophysical Observatory, 1891; Langley Aerodynamical Laboratory,
1913; American Historical Association materials, 1889;
National Gallery of Art and Freer Gallery.   See also
1875.

1846   The Mercantile Library Association is established
in St. Louis (EA 1957, v. 17, p. 356a).   See also 1818.

1846 Hoe patents a rotary printing press (Glaister p. 221). A great step toward cheaper printed books.

1847 John Edmands' Subjects for Debates, with References and Authorities is published by the Brothers in Unity Library, Yale (Williamson pp. 5-6). It is a definite forerunner of the Debaters' Handbook series.

1847 A.V. Blake American Booksellers' Complete Reference Trade List is published (Beswick p. 40); another attempt at trade bibliography.

1847 Propaganda move: the Boston City Council authorizes the acknowledgement of a gift of 50 books from the city of Paris (Shera p. 175); the mayor is instructed to make a suitable return gift. An earlier gift which could be classed as propagandistic was that of Louis XVI to Wm. and Mary College and the college in Pennsylvania in 1784, cf. Shores; even earlier, 1698, William III made a gift to King's Chapel, Boston (Shera p. 26) which must have been influenced by the recent death of Mary II and his desire to remain in the good graces of all his subjects.

1848 Poole publishes his first index to periodicals, An Alphabetical Index to Subjects Treated in Reviews, and Other Periodicals; it covers the entire periodical collection of the Brothers in Unity Library at Yale (Pettee p. 43).

1848 The earliest reported card catalog in the U.S. is begun in 1847 or 1848, at Harvard (AmLA 1960, p. 178).

1848 The earliest known legislative authorization for free public libraries by municipalities is granted to Boston by the Massachusetts General Court (Bostwick p. 8); in 1851 the law is extended to the entire state.

1848 The earliest known photographic reproduction of manuscripts is reported at the monastery on Mount Athos, by Sevastianof (LibT v. 5, no. 2, p. 266).

1849 Who's Who begins annual publication under St.

Martin's Press, New York (Shove p. 94).

1849   The New Hampshire "short law" is enacted for municipal support of public libraries (Joeckel p. 25).

1849   The Roorback Bibliotheca Americana is published (Rogers p. 6).

1849   By this date the Social Library is widespread in the U.S. (Joeckel p. 3), although enabling legislation is rapidly becoming popular in states desiring municipally supported public libraries.

1850   A classed catalog with an alphabetical index to subject entries is issued by the Philadelphia Mercantile Company (Ranz p. 58); influential in its attempts to solve the increasing problems of the classed catalog, see also 1843.   The New York Society Library prepares a similar catalog this same year, and a few other libraries followed the example in later years.

1850   The modern public library is defined by the Public Libraries Act of July 30, England, making possible libraries with unrestricted access, supported by fixed taxes and appropriations (Predeek p. 55).   In essence this is the U.S. definition also.

1850   Jewett proposes his famous but unsuccessful plan for centralized cataloging by using stereotype plates (USLC p. xi).

1850   "Ladies libraries" have become popular in the U.S. by this date (Joeckel p. 3).

1850   Jewett's list of "Copyright Publications" is added to the Smithsonian Report, a forerunner of the Catalogue of Copyright Entries (Rogers p. 23).

1850   A Federal library in the Department of the Interior is reported to begin this year (Johnson p. 354).

1850   Jewett presents his "Report on Public Libraries" in the Appendix to the Report of the Board of Regents

of the Smithsonian Institution (Ranz p. 100, note 3); issued as House Miscellaneous Publication, no. 50. See
also 1876, under surveys.

1850   The smallest movable type is cast by Giaco-
mo Gnocchi at Milan, called the "flies eyes, " about a
2-point; used in 1878 for an edition of La Divina Com-
mèdia (Spielmann p. 39).

1851   Jewett commends the work of the Sunday School
libraries in the U.S. (Shera p. 239, note 90).   England
had book service to the poor through its Sunday School
Union as early as 1803; these libraries in the U.S.
were more like Social Libraries.

1851   Essays and general literature indexing is begun
this year by Albert Hebard as an appendix to the Brothers in Unity Catalog, Yale (Williamson p. 6).

1851   The Norton's Literary Advertiser appears as a
supplement to the Bibliotheca Americana (Growoll p.
xxviii), important in the history of a U.S. national bibliography, cf. Rogers, p. 6.

1851   Micro-photography is furthered by Dancer and
others working with iodized collodion processes (LibT
v. 5, no. 2, p. 277).

1851   Fire destroys a portion of the LC holdings, including part of the Jeffersonian Library and most of the
copyright deposits (Rogers p. 29).

1852   Jewett's "Code of 39 rules" is included in his report On the Construction of Catalogues of Libraries
(Tauber p. 133).   Even at this date he was advocating
the dictionary catalog, cf. Pettee p. 32.

1852   The Boston Public Library is put under control
of a Board of Trustees, which Joeckel says is the earliest known and sets a precedent (Joeckel p. 20).

1852   The earliest reported YMCA library opens at Boston on March 11 (AmLA 1960, p. 178).

1852   Sidney Smirke designs the circular reading room for the British Museum, a factor in the history of library architecture (EB 1950, v. 14, p. 26).

1852   Fox Talbot discovers the chromate process, which leads to photogravure and cheaper photo-reproduction (Glaister pp. 66; 308).   This is a year for much work in the field of photo-lithography and reproduction for book illustration, cf. Glaister.

1853   Earliest reported attempts to form an association of librarians in the U. S. (Beswick p. 56).

1853   Blor proposes using photography as a method of reproducing a library catalog (USLC p. xi).   Anticipates by more than a hundred years our modern methods.   In 1964 the first computer-produced university library catalog is issued for Florida Atlantic University, Boca Raton, Fla., cf. LCIB v. 23, no. 42, p. 591.

1853   The Poole Index to Periodical Literature is first published under this title (Pettee p. 43).   Cf. Ranz, p. 115, notes 87; 89.   Before this date libraries had used analytics in the general catalogs to show contents of periodical literature.   See also 1848.

1853   The Mercantile Library Association is established in San Francisco (EA 1957, v. 17, p. 356a).   See also 1818.

1853   The Federal library in the Attorney General's Office is reported to begin this year (Johnson p. 354).

1853   An experiment this year in a multi-color process for printing gaily decorated boards for bookbinding is the beginning of "yellowbacks," cheap editions of popular literature (*Carter p. 148).

1854   Two forerunners of modern dictionary catalogs appear: Boston Public Library catalog prepared by Edward Capen and the Boston Mercantile Library catalog prepared by William F. Poole (Ranz pp. 48-49); in 1870 Poole supervises such a catalog for the Silas Bronson Library, and in 1871 for the Cincinnati Public.

1854 The earliest reported book stacks are designed by Labroust (his Magasin des imprimés) in Paris (EB 1950, v. 14, p. 26).

1854 The first true public library in the U.S. opens, the Boston Public (Bostwick p. 8). Cognizance should be taken of the municipal library of Wayland, Mass., opened in 1850, whose failure to be recognized as first may rest on a mere technicality, cf. Shera, pp. 189-191.

1854 Maine votes enabling legislation for municipal public libraries (Bostwick p. 8).

1854 The Astor Library opens in New York City (Thornton p. 197). Is now part of the New York Public.

1855 Bartlett's Familiar Quotations has its first edition this year (Shove p. 82).

1855 A Mechanics' Institute Library opens in San Francisco (EA 1957, v. 17, p. 356a). See also 1818.

1855 The American Publishers' Circular and Literary Gazette is published, an early attempt at trade bibliography in the U.S. (Growoll p. xxviii).

1856 The earliest reported employment of a woman librarian is that of Mrs. A. B. Harnden at the Boston Athenaeum (AmLA 1960, p. 178).

1856 The Shurtleff cataloging rules appear, a direct influence on the Dewey Decimal Classification (Dewey, ed. 16, Introd.).

1856 The Cincinnati Public Library is reported to open this year (EB ed. 11, v. 16, p. 564).

1857 The monumental catalog of the Astor Library is begun this year by Cogswell, and completed in 1866

(ALA 1932, p. 98).

1857 Esparto grass paper, for printing and writing, is produced in England at the Eynsham Mills, Oxford, under Thomas Routledge (+Hunter p. 363). See also 1869.

1857 The Mercantile Library Association in Brooklyn opens (Thornton p. 198). See also 1818.

1857 An endowed reference library opens at the George Peabody Institute, Baltimore (EA Reprint p. 357cc).

1857 The Mexican national library, La Biblioteca Nacional de Mexico at Mexico City, begins at this date (Esdaile p. 319).

1858 Jewell issues his Index to the Catalogue for the Boston Public (Pettee p. 32). It greatly furthers the movement toward the dictionary catalog: cross references, distinguishing author's names by dates, subject headings interfiled with authors and titles, cf. Ranz pp. 67-70. See also 1861. Two other catalogs prepared similarly were those of the Philadelphia Mercantile Library, 1870, and the Buffalo Young Men's Association Library, 1871.

1858 An endowed reference library opens, the David Watkinson Library, Hartford, Conn. (EA Reprint p. 357cc).

1858 Allibone's A Critical Dictionary of English Literature and British and American Authors is published in three volumes, 1858-1871 (*Altick p. 15); a supplement in two volumes is published in 1891.

1859 The issue of Sunday library service in public libraries is raised in Boston (Marshall p. 59).

1859 Deposit copies under the U.S. copyright law of 1790 begin to be made to the Department of Interior rather than to the Department of State (Rogers p. 12).

1859 The Worcester (Mass.) Public is reported to open

this year (EB ed. 11, v. 16, p. 564).

1859 An endowed reference library is founded, the Seth Grouvenor Library, Buffalo, N.Y. (EA Reprint p. 357 cc); it opens in 1870.

1860 The Department of Agriculture Library opens (Predeek p. 97). This is the forerunner of the U.S. National Agricultural Library, 1960.

1860 The U.S. Government Printing Office (GPO) is established by law, 12 Stat. 117, June 23 (Brown p. 5).

1861 One of the first and most widely acclaimed public card catalogs (manuscript) is opened at Harvard, prepared by Ezra Abbot and Cutter (Ranz p. 53); card catalogs were never opened to the public until the 1850's. This is another attempt at the alphabeticoclassed arrangement, cf. Ranz, pp. 60; 70-72. See also 1790.

1861 Further work toward the dictionary catalog is done by Jewett in his second Index to the Collection for the Boston Public (Pettee p. 32). See also 1858.

1861 The Italian national library, La Biblioteca Nazionale Centrale at Florence, begins this year, and assumes this name in 1885 (Esdaile p. 167); Italy has six other national depositories which are centers of historical collections: Rome 1875; Milan 1786; Naples 1804; Palermo ca 1782; Turin ca 1720; Venice ca 1553.

1861 The U.S. Military Post Library Association is organized (Johnson p. 356); by 1875 nearly every post or garrison had a library; after 1920 trained personnel were provided; by 1943 there was a network of libraries, here and overseas.

1862 Federal library: Post Office Department is reported to begin one this year (Johnson p. 354).

1862 The Russian national library, Lenin State Library at Moscow, opens to the public this year (Esdaile p. 240).

1864   LC prints a complete, alphabetical author catalog, the only one ever compiled by LC (Mearns p. 85); this was a departure from its classed catalogs, and was the first general LC catalog done by GPO, which had done the annual supplements since 1862.   See also 1869.

1864   The English Catalogue of Books begins publication (McKerrow p. 140).   The period 1801-1836 was covered in a volume published in 1914.

1864   The Statesman's Yearbook begins publication (Shove p. 44).

1865   The earliest reported course of library instruction is inaugurated at the University of Naples (White p. 67); in 1869 the Italian minister of public instruction began plans for a two-year diploma course in library science at university level, but it was never established.

1865   LC is reinstated as recipient of deposit copies under the copyright law, with penalties being set up (Rogers p. 31).

1865   Vermont gets enabling legislation for municipal public libraries (Bostwick p. 8).

1865   The Bullock press begins web printing from a continuous reel, early rotary form (Glaister p. 351).

1865   Egloffstein does early work with the screen process in reproduction of pictures (Glaister p. 168).   See also 1518; 1642.

1865   Two public libraries are reported to open this year: Detroit Public, and St. Louis Public (EB ed. 11, v. 16, p. 564).

1866   A printed catalog issued in parts is begun by the Boston Public, the first practical demonstration of this innovation, Cogswell having abandoned the plan for the Astor Library (Ranz p. 50).

1866   The U.S. Congress provides for removal of the

Smithsonian Library to LC (Mearns p. 102); the proposal first came in 1865; the actual moving was completed in 1867.

1866   The Kelly American Catalog of Books, volume
one, is published (Growoll p. xxxii); volume two was
published in 1871.

1866   The first published annual report of the Librarian
of Congress appears this year (Mearns p. 89).

1866   Henry Harrisse publishes his Bibliotheca Americana Vetustissima, 1493-1550, described now as the
first scholarly work in American bibliography (Bühler
p. 98).

1866   The last of the handmade paper mills in the U.S.
disappears this year (+Hunter p. 364).

1867   The first of the "library bulletins," an innovation
in printed catalogs, appears at the Boston Public under
Winsor (Ranz p. 51); in 1869 the Boston Athenaeum began issuing them; by 1876 the success of the bulletin
was assured as various public libraries adopted them.
The first college library bulletin was reported at Harvard in 1875, cf. AmLA 1957, p. 126.

1867   The earliest reported industrial library opens at
the Mallinckrodt Chemical Company, St. Louis (EA
1957, v. 17, p. 357r).

1867   Howard Challin publishes his Uniform Trade-list
Circular, another attempt at trade bibliography in the
U.S. (Beswick p. 40).

1867   Part One of the Sabin Dictionary of Books Relating to America is published (Growoll p. xxi); published
under full title Bibliotheca Americana, a Dictionary of
Books Relating to America from its Discovery to the
Present Time in 29 volumes, 1868-1936, it was continued by Wilberforce Eames and completed by R.W.G.
Vail, cf. *Carter, p. 174.

1867 The exchange program at LC receives new impetus as heir to the Smithsonian Library system of exchanges; Spofford asks for additional government documents; in 1884 a European agency is supplied to stimulate exchanges with foreign governments (Mearns pp. 104-105). See also 1840.

1867 Ohio gets enabling legislation for municipal public libraries (Bostwick p. 8).

1867 The Peter Force Historical Library is bought by LC this year for $100,000 (Mearns p. 108).

1868 Leypoldt begins publication of Literary Bulletin with the Christmas issue, a trade bibliography and news bulletin (Beswick p. 17).

1868 Earliest reported service-to-the-blind program in a U.S. library opens at the Boston Public with a gift of eight embossed volumes (EA 1957, v. 17, p. 356q).

1868 The World Almanac begins publication (Shove p. 43). Its British counterpart, Whitakers' Almanak, begins in 1868 or 1869, cf. Shove; Glaister.

1868 The Indianapolis Public is reported to open this year (EB ed. 11, v. 16, p. 564).

1868 The earliest known vertical file appears this year, one produced by Amberg File and Index Company (*Schellengerg p. 83); the Woodruff file cabinet or holder for folded documents in a sequential arrangement also is reported this year; in 1893 the Rosenau vertical file came on the market, sponsored by the Library Bureau.

1869 Leypoldt issues the first of his The American Educational Catalogue (Beswick p. 26).

1869 Howard Challin publishes his Publishers' and Stationers' Trade-list Directory, catalogs bound in original form (Beswick p. 40). A forerunner of PTLA.

1869 Esparto grass paper is reported to reach the U.S.

this year (+Hunter p. 363).

1869   The earliest reported legislation for "extension
services" from a U.S. library is the Vermont enact-
ment on rural library development, with authority to
contract for services (LibT v. 10, no. 2, p. 89).
AmLA reports extension services at Oxford began in
1878, cf. AmLA 1964, p. 201.

1869   An example of the alphabetico-classed catalog is
issued by LC in its Index to Subjects, complementing
its full author catalog (Ranz p. 72).   Cf. Mearns p.
117.   See also 1864.

1869   The earliest reported University Press in the
U.S. is established at Cornell University, from 1869 to
1884 (Kerr p. 16).   See also 1878.

1869   The Cleveland Public is reported to open this
year (EB ed. 11, v. 16, p. 564).

1870   LC begins to receive all deposit copies required
by the U.S. copyright law, and to administer the copyright law (Rogers pp. 12; 31).

1870   Contribution to library education: Emerson's essay on Books (White p. 65).

1870   Federal library: Office of Education is reported
to open one this year (EA 1953, v. 17, p. 357a).

1870   Leypoldt issues monthly book lists with indices,
under title The American Catalogue of Books for 1869
(Beswick p. 24).

1871   Free Public Libraries, published in brochure
form by the American Social Science Association, is the
first formal treatise on the subject in the U.S. (Wyer
p. 3).

1871   The earliest reported branch library in the U.S.
opens at East Boston, Mass. (AmLA 1960, p. 178).
Bostwick gives the date as 1870.   Shera says that the

"coonskin" library of Ames, Ohio had a branch as
early as 1811, cf. Shera, p. 193, note 104. Predeek
reports that the first branch libraries for England were
at Manchester in 1857.

1871 Propaganda move: England sends books to Chicago to help rebuild the library destroyed by the great
fire (EA 1957, v. 17, p. 356).

1872 The Chicago Public is founded after the fire of
1871, and opens this year (Thornton p. 201). The Los
Angeles Public is reported to open this year (EA 1957,
v. 17, p. 366w).

1872 Illinois passes the "long law," a detailed municipal library act making the library independent of the
city council except for tax subsidy (Joeckel p. 25).

1872 The earliest reported use of a printed card catalog is that of Winsor at the Boston Public (AmLA 1957,
p. 126). This was the beginning of Winsor's unique
"pasted card," an idea he borrowed from Leyden University; it was adopted by the St. Louis Public School
Library, and the New York Public in 1896, cf. Ranz;
Pettee.

1872 The Japanese national library, National Diet Library at Tokyo, begins this year (Esdaile p. 386).

1873 The Dewey Decimal Classification System is first
used, at Amherst College (Tauber p. 190).

1873 The Congressional Record begins publication with
the first session of the fifty-third Congress (Shove p.
103). It was preceded by the Annals of Congress, 1789-
1824; the Register of Debates, 1824-1837; and the Congressional Globe, 1833-1873.

1873 The Publishers' Weekly begins publication under
that title (Beswick p. 28); in 1869 a forerunner appeared in the Trade Circular and Literary Bulletin.

1873 The Uniform Trade List Annual begins, a binding

of publishers' catalogs (Beswick p. 41); in 1874 it assumed the title Publishers' Trade List Annual, the PTLA or "green pig." See also 1869.

1873 Leypoldt begins issuing his Monthly Book Circular, another link in the history of U.S. trade bibliography (Beswick p. 20).

1874 Cutter begins his Catalogue of the Library of the Boston Athenaeum, 1807-1871, in five volumes, to be completed in 1882 (Pettee p. 35). This was a triumph for Cutter and the dictionary catalog in the U.S.; note should be made of its use of true subject entries, cross references, analytics; the work actually began under Poole in 1856, was continued 1862-1870 by Charles R. Lowell, cf. Ranz, pp. 73-75.

1874 Poole produces the first of his famous "finding lists," devised to keep the printed catalogs up-to-date at the least expenditure (Ranz p. 92); by the end of the nineteenth century they were widely used in the U.S., but finally gave way to the printed card.

1874 Contribution to library education: Frederick Rullmann, Library Science as a Special University Study in Germany, published as a brochure (White p. 86).

1874 Coated paper is first used for book printing (Sutermeister p. 170). Hunter gives the date as 1875; and that it was made by Charles Gage for DeVinne, cf. +Hunter.

1875 By this date it is agreed by most librarians that a catalog must give information concerning author, title, and subject of every book, cf. Ranz, p. 39.

1875 Robert Barclay opens the way to modern offset printing by using a cylinder covered with card paper to print on tin (Glaister p. 285).

1875 The Milwaukee Public is reported to open this year (EB ed. 11, v. 16, p. 564).

1875   The Smithsonian Institute begins publication of its
Bulletin series (Kainen p. vi); in 1878 it begins to publish its Proceedings; in 1902, its series, Contributions
from the U.S. National Herbarium. Its Annual Report
dates from 1846; its international exchange program
from 1867.

1876   The first national library association in the U.S.
holds its first conference, October 6, at Philadelphia
(Utley p. 11).   The American Library Association (ALA)
is organized, incorporated in 1879.   The Library Association of the United Kingdom was organized in 1877.

1876   Dewey's classification scheme is published under
title A Classification and Subject Index for Cataloging
and Arranging the Books and Pamphlets of a Library
(Ranz p. 111, note 36); the term "Relative Index" appears in all later titles, except the 1951.

1876   The Library Bureau of ALA is established (Thornton p. 202).

1876   A regional union list of periodicals is begun in
Baltimore (Downs p. 7); reported as one of the earliest
lists in the U.S.

1876   The first official survey of public libraries in the
U.S. is contained in the Special Report of the U.S. Bureau of Education published this year (Pettee p. 33).
Previous unofficial surveys had been made as follows:
1724, Bishop of London for Maryland; 1799-1818, Benjamin Trumbull for Connecticut; 1839, Horace Mann for
Massachusetts; 1845, Herman Ludwig's survey of American libraries; 1849, Henry Barnard for Rhode Island;
1851, Jewett's Notices of Public Libraries in the United
States; 1859, William J. Rhee's Manual of Public Libraries; 1859, Edward Edwards, Memoirs of Libraries,
cf. LibQ v. 5, no. 1, pp. 5ff.

1876   Cutter publishes his Rules for a Printed Dictionary Catalogue (Pettee p. 47); considered the first code
for complete cataloging.

1876   A forerunner of the modern "divided" catalog is seen in Jacob Schwartz's discussion of the catalog for the New York Apprentices' Library (Ranz pp. 72-73).

1876   The American Library Journal begins publication as the official journal of ALA (Beswick p. 55); later shortened to Library Journal (LJ).

1876   A telegraph is first proposed for library use at the British Museum (Garnett p. 257); a proposal to use a printing telegraph to transmit requests for books from the main desk to stack area.

1877   The first international library conference is held in London (Thornton p. 203); the Library Association of the United Kingdom begins this year.

1877   Library education is on the agenda of the first international library conference (see above), London (White p. 67).

1877   The earliest known proposal to mechanize library processes is one for using a typewriter (LibT v. 5, no. 2, p. 194).   The Sholes and Glidden was patented in 1868 and put on the market by Remington in 1873; the proposal to use it in technical processes comes at the New York Conference this year and is again discussed at the Lake George Conference in 1885.   Cf. Schultheiss. See also 1714; 1903.

1877   Stephen B. Noyes begins his catalog of the Brooklyn Mercantile Library, a modified alphabetico-classed arrangement without scientific basis, but most usable by the general public and widely praised by colleagues; it was completed in 1880 and copied for public libraries in 1878 by Edward Copen and in 1882 by Frederick B. Perkins (Ranz pp. 80-82).

1877   The Dewey system is completely applied for the first time to a large general library by Josephus Larned at the Buffalo Young Men's Association Library (Ranz p. 83).   See also 1873; 1879.

1877 A special Documents Committee is appointed by
ALA; in 1881 it recommended the annual issuance of a
list of all publications printed by authority of government bodies; the present system of listing and indexing
is a result of this cooperative interest (Ranz p. 96).

1877 Edison develops the first equipment capable of
recording and reproducing sound (Doss p. 176); the
first experiments in recording sound were reported as
early as 1859, using hog's bristles and lamp black.
Recognition must be given the work of the Bell Labora-
tories, 1881; with Edison's experiments, it led to the
talking-book, the Dictaphone and other inventions useful to libraries.

1877 The National Library of Ireland opens this year
(Esdaile p. 128); it evolved from the Library of the
Royal Dublin Society founded in 1815.

1878 The first proposal is made by ALA for a cooperative plan of centralized cataloging, to be administered from the offices of Publishers' Weekly (Ranz p. 98);
it lasts only one year.

1878 The Trustees of the Public Library of the City
of Boston are given full powers over library and property (Joeckel p. 21); this forms a precedent for U.S.
public libraries.

1878 The Providence Public is reported to open this
year (EB ed. 11, v. 16, p. 564).

1878 The National Library of Bulgaria, Vassil Kolarov
State Library at Sofia, begins this year (Esdaile p. 267).

1878 The Johns Hopkins Press is the oldest continuous
university press in the U.S. (Sears p. 4); basing its
claim on a beginning this year as the Publication Agency
to produce the American Journal of Mathematics. See
also French. Other university presses in the U.S. appear: 1869, Cornell, which see; 1892, Chicago; 1893,
California and Columbia; 1905, Princeton; 1908, Yale;
1913, Harvard; 1922, North Carolina (claims to be the

first State university press), and Texas (reorganized in 1950); 1927, Minnisota, cf. French; Sears; Minn.

1879 The Index Medicus begins publication under Leypoldt (Pettee p. 45); planned by John Shaw Billings to supplement the Surgeon-General's Library Catalog. In 1960 it was taken over by the National Library of Medicine, cf. Schmeckebier, p. 76. Computerized processes for indexing grow out of a project to begin in 1960; the MEDLARS program was officially launched in 1961, cf. LDAP pp. 111; 117.

1879 The Cutter Expansive Classification is first published in the Library Journal, this year (Thornton p. 203).

1879 The Schwartz Mnemonic System of Classification is published this year (Thornton p. 203).

1879 The second proposal from ALA for a cooperative plan for centralized cataloging is made; the "Title Slip Registry" is to be supplied as a supplement to the Library Journal (Ranz p. 98); it fails within a year.

1879 The first attempts are made at a cataloging-in-source program, a cooperative venture (USLC p. xvi); this attempt was discontinued in 1880; it was first proposed in 1876 that cataloging information be printed in the book, cf. USLC, p. xii.

1879 The earliest reported "open shelves" in U.S. libraries begin at Pawtucket, R.I. Free Library (Bostwick p. 9). AmLA reports the first at Beaver Dam, Wisconsin, in 1885; Bostwick says that after 1895, when the Free Library of Philadelphia adopted the practice, "open access" spread rapidly. Predeek says that England adopted the practice in 1894 at Clerkenwell Public; Thornton says Truro had open shelves for eight years prior to this date. This diversity of opinion probably can be accounted for in the interpretation of "open access" and "open shelves. "

1879 Linderfelt applies the Dewey system to the Milwaukee Public Library, on a card catalog; in 1885 it was printed, one of the first examples of printed catalogs classed according to Dewey, cf. Ranz, p. 83. See also 1873; 1877.

1879   The Statistical Abstract of the United States begins publication under the U.S. Bureau of the Census (Shove p. 64).

1879   The Grove's Dictionary of Music and Musicians begins publication in London, 1879-1889 (Shove p. 79).

1880   John Shaw Billings begins his Index-Catalogue of the Library of the Surgeon-General's Office, published 1880-1895, the first in a series of comprehensive alphabetical catalogs, continued until 1948 (Pettee p. 45). Note should be made of the number of analytical entries cf. Ranz, pp. 79-80.   See also 1874.

1880   The Leypoldt American Catalogue, volume one, is published (Growoll p. lxxiv).   A first installment was done by Armstrong in 1878, cf. Beswick, p. 47.

1880   Punched cards and equipment for manipulating them are first used in mechanical computation by Hollerith, for the U.S. census (Casey p. 4).

1880   Earliest reported use of pictorial end-sheets (+Hunter p. 368).   The prototype of this was the "doublure," the fine leather or watered silk lining of Italian or French Jansenist binding, about 1550, cf. Glaister; *Carter.

1880   Ayers' Directory of newspapers and periodicals in the U.S. and Canada begins publication (Hower p. 83); it is first known under title American Newspaper Annual.

1881   Andrew Carnegie donates a library to Pittsburgh, Penn., cf. Kull.   He also gives libraries to Dunfermline, Scotland, and Allegheny, Penn.; these were not part of his endowment program, which had to be matched by the townships, but outright gifts.   See also 1889.

1882   A new edition of Poole's Index appears, a cooperative venture first proposed to ALA in 1876 (Ranz p.
96).   See also 1848; 1853.

1882   The earliest reported music library in the U.S.
opens at the Brooklyn Public (AmLA 1960, p. 178).

1882   A Federal library: the Geological Survey is reported to open one this year (EB ed. 11, v. 16, p.
562).   Its Bibliography of North American Geology begins 1886; the Professional Papers, 1902; the Geophysi-
cal Abstracts, 1929.

1882   The Halkett and Laing A Dictionary of the Anonymous and Pseudonymous Literature of Great Britain,
published in four volumes 1882-1888, first appears
(*Carter p. 109); in 1926 a new edition was prepared
by Smith and Johnson, in seven volumes; in 1956 volume 8, to cover 1900-1950, was prepared by Rhodes
and Simoni; a supplement is now in preparation.

1882   The Enoch Pratt Library, Baltimore, is reported
to open this year (Thornton p. 204).

1883   The Catalogue of the Library of the Peabody Institute is begun, and completed in five volumes in 1892,
described now as the most complete and finest of American printed alphabetical catalogs (Pettee p. 33).   From
1896 to 1905 an even fuller work was published in eight
volumes; note should be made of the analytical entries
used, cf. Ranz, pp. 78-80.   See also 1874; 1880.

1883   The first ALA rules for standard cataloging are
issued (ALA 1932, p. 98).   Based on Jewett, these
ALA Condensed Rules for an Author and Title Catalog
are first published in the Library Journal; later they
are reprinted in Cutter's Rules.   Thornton says that
English rules are published this year by the Bodleian,
with the Library Association, cf. Thornton, p. 205.

1883   The Co-operative Index to Periodicals is prepared
by W.I. Fletcher (Lawler p. 38).

1883   Leypoldt issues Library Aids, a forerunner of
Library Annual (Beswick pp. 58-59).

1883   A formal course in Bibliography is offered at the
University of Michigan (AmLA 1961, p. 179); which is
thought to be the first of its kind in the U.S.

1884   Mergenthaler invents the Linotype typesetting machine (Glaister p. 254); the New York Tribune used the
first successful model in 1886.   In 1890 the inventor
perfected his machine; the first library user was probably the New London (Conn.) Public, in 1891, printing
its "finding list"; in 1892, the Boston Public used it;
in 1893, the Enoch Pratt Free Library, cf. Ranz, p.
86.

1884   The first formal library education program is
tested by Dewey in preliminary classes (White p. 62);
handwriting is a part of the curriculum.

1884   The Engineering Index begins an annual indexing
and abstracting service (Shove p. 71).

1884   The New English Dictionary (NED) begins in in-
stallments, under the editorship of Sir James Murray;
it was finished in 1928 (Shove p. 33, note).   In 1933 it
assumed the title Oxford English Dictionary (OED) when
reissued in thirteen volumes.   In 1836 the English work
New Dictionary of English Language of Charles Richardson (issued in two volumes, 1836-1837) was a great step
in dictionary history.

1885   The Dictionary of National Biography (DNB) begins publication under Smith, Elder (Shove p. 95).

1885   The Poore Descriptive Catalogue is published
(Powell p. 25).   This is reported to be the first check-
list of U.S. government publications, and covers from
September 5, 1774 to March 4, 1881.

1885   The earliest reported separate children's room in
a U.S. library opens in New York City under Hanaway
(Bostwick p. 11).   Lucas reports the first one as of

1895; the Encyclopaedia Britannica reports one for the
Brookline (Mass.) Public in 1890. Thornton says the
earliest known such room in England was at Nottingham
in 1882, cf. Thornton, p. 204.

1885 The Minneapolis Public is reported to open this
year (EB ed. 11, v. 16, p. 564).

1886 George Watson Cole produces a catalog for the
Fitchburg (Mass.) Public with a main classified sequence that is a faithful reproduction of the Dewey classification (Ranz p. 84). See also 1877; 1879.

1886 The ALA Publishing Section is organized (*Dewey
p. 103).

1886 Dziatzko devises his influential rules for cataloging (Tauber p. 133); in 1890 Linderfelt translated them
and published the Eclectic Card Catalog Rules.

1886 Dewey begins his journal Library Notes, used as
a textbook at the Albany School (White p. 98).

1887 The first U.S. Library School, the School of Library Economy, opens at Columbia University, under
Dewey as Professor of Library Economy (White p. 80);
in 1880 the Library Association, England, began its
first considerations for education; England's first school
opened at University College, London, in 1919, a two-
year course, cf. Predeek, p. 78. Schools for training
"keepers" are alleged to exist in Babylonia as early as
3200 B.C., and the origin of library schools may lie
in the initiation ceremonies of primitive tribes, which
taught the young men the use of message sticks, etc.,
cf. Richardson, pp. 133; 142.

1887 ALA's third plan for a cooperative program of
centralized cataloging: its Publishing Section announces
a plan for supplying cards for annual selection of books
(Ranz p. 98); it fails for lack of response.

1887 International copyright: Berne Convention convenes (Nicholson p. 5). Nicholson and Glaister say

1887; Steinberg says 1886. The "Berne Union" consists of the original convention plus successive revisions of Paris, Berlin, Rome, Brussels, cf. Walls.

1887 Compact shelving is foreseen in the "sliding presses" introduced this year at the British Museum (Garnett p. 267). They were first observed at Bethnal Green Free Library in 1886, an invention of Dr. Tyler to house patents; some earlier experiments had been made at Bradford Free Library, cf. +Esdaile, p. 138. The Library of the IAEA, Vienna, is using now (1966) an efficient modern version of this form of compact shelving.

1887 The Newberry Library, Chicago, opens (EA Reprint p. 357cc). The bequest for a free reference library was made in 1868.

1887 The Sonnenschein Best Books is first published (Sonnenschein, v. 1, "Notes").

1887 The Pratt Institute Free Library, Brooklyn, is reported to open this year (EA Reprint p. 357cc).

1889 The National Association of State Libraries is organized as a Division of ALA (AmLA 1958, p. 25); in 1898 it became a separate entity.

1889 The first reported technical division in a library opens at Carnegie Library, Pittsburgh (Predeek p. 105).

1889 The degrees BLS, MLS, and DLS are established at the Albany School (White p. 95).

1889 The Columbia Library School moves to the State Library in Albany, N.Y., and assumes the name, Albany School (White p. 92).

1889 The first ALA committee on Library Schools is appointed (White p. 153).

1889 The earliest reported legislation establishing a traveling library is enacted in New York State this year

(Bostwick p. 17). Bostwick says there was a "revolving" library that "traveled" between Kittery and York, Maine; Shera dates this at 1751, cf. Shera, p. 52.

1889 A classification scheme for the U.S. Department of Agriculture Library is devised by W.I. Fletcher (EA 1953, v. 17, p. 357s).

1889 The Newark (N.J.) Public is reported to open this year (EB ed. 11, v. 16, p. 564).

1889 An endowed reference library opens, the Howard Memorial Library at New Orleans (EA Reprint p. 357cc).

1889 The earliest "Carnegie" library, i.e., one under an endowment which had to be matched by the township, is reported to open at Braddock, Penn. this year (AmLA 1964, p. 202). See also 1881.

1889 The Association of College and Research Libraries (ACRL) has its beginning this year (AmLA 1958, p. 15), in a meeting of thirteen libraries at St. Louis (the R stood for Reference); in 1897 it became an ALA section; in 1938, an entity in its own right; 1947, acquired its own headquarters at ALA; 1955, began its grants to academic libraries. See also 1939; 1952; 1953.

1889 The Library begins publication this year (*Altick p. 69); in 1920 it merged with the Transactions (1893) of the Bibliographical Society (Eng.).

1890 The earliest reported U.S. State Library Commission (Drury p. 264); the Massachusetts Free Public Library commission, first library extension agency, cf. AmLA 1960, p. 179.

1890 The earliest reported Legislative Reference Service in the U.S. begins at the New York State Library (Drury p. 441).

1890 Reference service: a method for recording reference citations is noted in LJ for July (LibT v. 12, no. 3, p. 374). A new attention is being given to referral

122

services in the public library. Re citations see 731.

1890 The American Association of Library Trustees is organized (AmLA 1958, p. 4).

1890 A Library School opens at Pratt Institute, Brooklyn, N.Y. (AmLA 1959, p. 179).

1891 The "Rudolph Indexer," a facility for the simultaneous viewing of many entries in a library catalog, is first introduced at the ALA Conference; by 1898 it has proved itself inadequate (Ranz p. 89).

1891 The earliest reported circulating picture library opens at the Denver Public (AmLA 1960, p. 179).

1891 Apprentice classes open at the Los Angeles Public for training librarians (White p. 149); became influential throughout the U.S.

1891 Reference service: the term "reference work" first appears in the L.J. Index for October (LibT v. 12, no. 3, p. 374). See also 1890.

1891 The Chase Act extends copyright protection to foreign authors publishing in the U.S. (Nicholson p. 7).

1891 Copyright deposit lists are authorized by the U.S. government (Rogers p. 46); the Catalogue of Title-entries begins as a serial publication. See also 1906.

1891 The Philadelphia Free Library is reported to open this year (EB ed. 11, v. 16, p. 564).

1891 A School of Library Science opens at Drexel Institute of Technology, Philadelphia (AmLA 1959, p. 178).

1891 A summer school course in library education is held at Amherst College under William I. Fletcher (White p. 129).

1892 A union list of serials is published in California, the forerunner of such lists in the U.S. (Downs p. 7).

1892   The foundations for the Institute Internationale du
Bibliographie are laid in Brussels this year by Paul
Otlet and Henri LaFontaine (LibT v. 1, no. 2, p. 191).
See also 1895.   The "documentalist" is just appearing
on the horizon of U.S. librarianship; Irwin tells us that
in Bacon's New Atlantis, which described the college of
scientific research and some of the Fellows engaged in
collecting abstracts for it, these Fellows were called
"merchants of light, " which today would be translated
as documentalists or information officers, cf. Wormald,
p. 11.

1893   The Catalog of "ALA" Library is first published,
a cooperative venture in book selection cataloged at the
New York State Library (Cooper p. 9); other editions
appeared in 1904, 1912, and 1926.   It was first proposed by Dewey at ALA Conference in 1877, cf. Ranz,
p. 97.   See also 1904.

1893   The earliest reported traveling library begins in
New York State (Bostwick p. 17).   See also 1889.

1893   A World Library Congress is held at the Colum-
bian Exposition in Chicago this year (ALA 1929, p. 94).

1893   Reference service: personal assistance in library
reference work is first projected (Wyer p. 4); a government survey on libraries includes a reference to "personal assistance" and Wyer attributes to it the first
conception of the idea in relation to library reference
service.   In this same year specialized reference workers are found at the public libraries of Boston, Providence, Milwaukee, Detroit, Newark, Chicago, St. Louis
and Brooklyn (LibT v. 12, no. 3, p. 374).

1893   The ALA Index to General Literature is first published by its Publishing Board, with W.I. Fletcher as
editor, a cooperative venture; first proposed at ALA
Conference in 1882 by Poole (Ranz p. 96).   In 1905 a
second edition is published; in 1914, a supplement; it
is superseded by the Essay and General Literature Index, cf. Shove, p. 84.   See also 1931.

1893   A printed card program is proposed by the Rudolph Indexer Company to supply cards for all books currently published in the U. S., Cutter to be in charge (Ranz p. 98); the plan never materialized.

1893   A similar printed card program is proposed this year by the Library Bureau of ALA; in 1896 the Publishing Section assumed responsibility, but the plan was never truly successful (Ranz pp. 98-99); in 1900 a new trial of the plan was proposed by the ALA Co-operative Committee, but the beginning of the LC card distribution program made the ALA program unnecessary.

1893   A Library School is founded at Armour Institute of Technology, Urbana, Ill. (White p. 144); in 1897 it moved to the University of Illinois; in 1911 it advanced to graduate level.

1894   Earliest reported children's department in a U. S. public library opens at the Denver Public this year (Am-LA 1960, p. 179).   The first separate building for a children's library is reported at Brooklyn in 1914, cf. EA Reprint p. 357g.

1894   A motion picture deposit is begun at LC (LCIB v. 23, no. 2, p. 16); the "paper prints" or contact prints are deposited for copyright, cf. QuarJ v. 21, no. 4.   See also item under 1958.

1895   The International Federation for Documentation (FID) evolves from the Institute Internationale du Bibliographie of Otlet and LaFontaine (AmLA 1958, p. 38). See also 1892.

1895   The New York Public Library is formed by consolidation of the Astor and the Lenox libraries, with the Tilden Trust (EA Reprint p. 357x).   Its Bulletin begins publication in 1897.

1895   The ALA List of Subject Headings for Use in Dictionary Catalogs is first issued; it will have three editions (Pettee p. 48).   The first proposal for such a list was made at the ALA Conference, 1892.

1895   The first serious work with photo-duplication in libraries is begun by FID (LibT v. 5, no. 2, p. 267).

1895   The U.S. Congress sets up a system of distribution of U.S. government documents to selected depository libraries (EA 1957, v. 17, p. 356d).

1895   The Office of the Superintendent of Documents is established and a general printing law enacted for government printing practices (Schmeckebier p. 6).

1895   The Public Documents Library is established (Schmeckebier p. 17).

1895   The University of Wisconsin opens a summer school course for library education (White p. 129).

1895   The U.S. Historical MSS Commission for the preservation of archival collections of private papers is established (Schellenberg p. 21).

1895   The Swiss national library, La Bibliothèque Nationale Suisse at Berne, begins this year (Esdaile p. 121).

1895   The Monthly Catalog begins its listing of U.S. government publications (Schmeckebier p. 117).

1895   The American Book Prices Current is first published (Thornton p. 208). Book Prices Current, London, began in 1888.

1895   The Yearbook of Agriculture is first issued by the U.S. Department of Agriculture (Shove p. 73).

1896   The Document Catalog of the U.S. Superintendent of Documents begins publication by the GPO (Shove p. 105); it is continued until 1945, and covers 1893-1940.

1896   The Dayton Public opens one of the early successful in-service training programs for librarians, under Electra C. Doren (White p. 136); by 1905 there is an assortment of training programs in the U.S.

1896   The Cumulative Index to Periodicals begins, prepared by W.H. Brett at the Cleveland Public (Lawler
p. 38).   It combines with the Readers' Guide in 1905,
cf. Readers' Guide 1900-1904, p. viii.

1896   International copyright: Paris Convention convenes (Walls p. 62).   See item under 1887.

1897   The librarian at LC is given complete control of
the library proper (Mearns p. 136).

1897   The John Crerar Library, Chicago, opens (EA
Reprint p. 357cc).   It was established in 1889.

1897   Recording sound onto flat discs, credited to Emil
Berliner, is perfected to commercial standards this
year (Doss p. 177); in the 1920's electronic amplifica-
tion improved these recordings; in the 1930's "long-
play" discs became possible.

1897   The Brown Adjustable Classification is issued
(Predeek p. 68).

1897   A copyright office is established at LC, with
Thorvold Solberg as the Register (Rogers p. 48).

1897   The LC Division of Music is organized (+Thomp-
son p. 1011).

1897   The Buffalo Public~~s reported to open this year
(Drury p. 118).

1897   Luxembourg's national library, La Bibliothèque
Nationale at Luxembourg, begins this year (Esdaile p.
163); it evolved from a royal library of 1798.

1897   The Catalogue Genérale des Livres Imprimés de
la Bibliothèque Nationale: Auteurs begins publication
this year (*Altick p. 43).

1898   The Cumulative Book Index (CBI) begins under
the H.W. Wilson Company (Glaister p. 93).   Since 1929
it has listed all the books printed in English, cf. Law-

ler p. 28).

1898   LC begins evening hours, assuming its role as
a reference library (Mearns p. 156).   In 1962 it began
a new, broader type of reference service, the National
Referral Center for Science and Technology, established with support from the National Science Foundation.

1898   Library education courses in "special libraries, "
i. e. law, medicine, etc. , are proposed (White p. 96).
The first formal courses were inaugurated at Columbia
School only in 1933.

1898   The Medical Library Association is organized
(AmLA 1960, p. 24).

1898   Magnetic recording is proved possible by Volde-
mar Poulsen, Denmark (Doss p. 181); development of
practical equipment is delayed until the 1930's.

1898   Robert Proctor begins issuing his Index to the
Early Printed Books in the British Museum (*Carter p.
156); this contained his famous classification system,
Proctor's Order, which made him one of the greatest
of incunabulists.

1898   The American Art Annual begins publication; in
1952 it became the American Art Directory (Shove p.
77).

1898   The Washington, D. C. Public is reported to open
this year (EB ed. 11, v. 16, p. 564).

1899   Alexander J. Rudolph proposes his "blueprint"
method, a photographic method for reproducing a printed catalog (Ranz p. 88).

1899   The first successful story-telling programs in
U. S. public libraries begin this year (LibT v. 12 no. 1,
p. 55) at the West End Branch of the Carnegie Library,
Pittsburgh, and at the Buffalo Public.

1899   The first of the United States Catalogue (U. S.

Cat.) series appears (Beswick p. 50). Others appear in 1902 and 1912, the last in 1928.

1899 The Josephson List of Union Lists of Periodicals is published (Downs p. 7).

1899 The Carnegie Library, San Juan, Puerto Rico, is organized as a public library (EA Reprint p. 349).

1899 The U.S. Public Archives Commission is established (Schellenberg p. 23) for the preservation of public papers; during the Colonial Period the collecting and preserving of archival materials was in the hands of individuals; after the Federal Government began, it passed to historical societies and some libraries; the interest shown by libraries was stimulated by Jared Sparks at Harvard, Peter Force at LC (1867), and George Bancroft at the Lenox Library (1893); the first inventory of federal archives in the U.S. was as late as 1904, by Leland and Van Tyne under the auspices of the Department of Historical Research, Carnegie Institution. Cf. Schellenberg, passim.

1899 Who's Who in America begins biennial publication under Marquis (Shove p. 93).

1900's

1900 The Dana Report on library education and recruitment is given at the ALA Conference, Montreal (White p. 189).

1900 A Children's Section is organized at ALA (Lucas p. 5); less than one hundred members showed interest at this time.

1900 The Alaska Public Library opens this year (Colby p. xxxii).

1900 The earliest known true "regional" union list is reported at Zurich, Switzerland (Downs p. 5).

1900 The American Booksellers Association is organized (Glaister p. 6).

1900   The Newark Charging System is presented by
Dana at the Newark Public (Geer p. 5). The century
begins with one of our most ambitious schemes, a
charging system which replaces a brave but inefficient
list of systems, including the ledger, the dummy, the
indicator, the temporary slip and the permanent slip.
Dana's system was very influential and like the others
was devised to get the book safely back to the library
on time. An interesting story is told by Esdaile of one
Cuspinian, who borrowed various precious manuscripts
from the Corvina, the library of Matthias Corvinus; in
1526 the Corvina fell into the hands of the Turks, except for the "overdues" held by Cuspinian--in which
there may hang some kind of a moral!

1900   Somewhere around this date Wouter Nijhoff, in
Holland, coined the useful term "post-incunabula, "
meaning certain printed books between 1501-1540 (*Carter p. 152); about 1920 Stephen Gaselee adopted it in
England to cover dates 1501-1520.

1901   A committee on standard rules for cataloging is
appointed by ALA (Tauber p. 134).

1901   A Library School opens at Carnegie Institute of
Technology, Pittsburgh(AmLA 1959, p. 178).   In 1964
it was reorganized as the Graduate School of Library
and Information Sciences, cf. LCIB, v. 23, no. 23, p.
267.

1901   The earliest known training school for children's
librarians is reported at the Carnegie Tech. Library
School (Lucas p. 5).

1901   LC begins its service of the printed catalog card
and centralized cataloging (Coates p. 65).

1901   LC begins a program of inter-library loan service (Mearns p. 175).

1901   The first Nobel awards are made, in Stockholm,

December 10; the fund for the annual prizes was established in 1896, by the will of Alfred Bernhard Nobel, cf. Columbia Encyclopedia, ed. 1942.

1901 A dictionary catalog for LC is prepared by Hanson (Mearns p. 173). Pettee says it is the most influential of the U.S. dictionary catalogs, cf. Pettee, p. 34.

1901 The LC classification system is published (Tauber p. 201).

1901 The Readers' Guide begins its indexing service under the H.W. Wilson Company (Lawler p. 165).

1902 The LC card copy program begins with receipt of copy from the Washington, D.C. libraries (Tauber p. 123). See also 1910.

1902 LC plans for depository libraries of the printed card service (Mearns p. 178).

1902 The Albany School requires a degree for admission and becomes the first graduate library school in the U.S. (White p. 99).

1902 A School of Library Science opens at Simmons College, Boston (AmLA 1959, p. 179).

1902 Kroeger edits the first guide to reference books, forerunner of Mudge and Winchell, under title Guide to the Study and Use of Reference Books (Wyer p. 14).

1902 The first work with the Photostat is done by G.C. Beidler, Oklahoma City (LibT v. 5, no. 2, p. 270). See also 1912.

1902 The "Grolier List" or "Grolier Hundred" is published under the title One Hundred Books Famous in English Literature (*Carter p. 105); it is issued by the Grolier Club, New York.

1902 The Times Literary Supplement (TLS) begins publication in London (*Altick p. 71).

1903   The earliest known theatre library in the U.S.
opens at Harvard, the Lowe Theatrical Library (EA
1957, v. 17, p. 357r).

1903   Typing courses are added to the library education curriculum of the Albany School (White p. 96).
Handwriting courses are continued in case there should
be a breakdown of the typewriter!

1903   The classed catalog of the Carnegie Library,
Pittsburgh, appears, prepared by Margaret Mann (Ranz
p. 84).

1903   Pi Lambda Sigma is organized at Syracuse University, to promote interest in library service (AmLA
1959, p. 180).

1903   The Charles Evans American Bibliography 1903-
1934, in twelve volumes, begins publication (Rogers p.
9).

1903   The first volume of Book-Auction Records, dated
from June, 1902, is published (Glaister p. 37).   In
1940-1951 the United States Cumulative Book Auction
Records was published, New York.

1904   The earliest known business library service in
the U.S. is reported at the Newark Public (AmLA 1960,
p. 179).

1904   The earliest known circulating collection of prints
and framed pictures is reported at the Newark Public
(AmLA 1960, p. 179).

1904   A Library School opens at the University of Wisconsin, Madison (AmLA 1959, p. 179).

1904   The John Carter Brown Library opens (EA 1953,
v. 17, p. 357cc).   A library of Americana begun by the
Brown family in the eighteenth century, now owned by
Brown University, see also 1767.

1904   LC publishes the ALA Catalog, 8,000 Volumes
for a Popular Library (Mearns p. 181).   This one is
edited by Dewey, with the cataloging done at the New
York State Library.   See also 1893.

1904   The U.S. Congress authorizes free mailing for
library service to the blind programs (EA 1957, v. 17,
p. 356q).

1904   The Bibliographical Society of America is organized (Rogers p. 34).   AmLA 1958 gives the date as
1906; its Papers (PBSA) begin in 1904, cf. *Carter.

1904   The first reported appearance of hand-sorted
punched cards is in this year (Casey p. 4).

1904   Rubel and Hermann discover that offset will print
on paper (Glaister p. 361); a successful machine for
lithographic printing on a rotary press appeared in 1899,
cf. Glaister, p. 107.

1904   Patterson's American Educational Directory begins
publication as an annual directory (Shove p. 57).

1904   The Granger Index to Poetry and Recitations is
first published this year (Winchell p. 374).   In 1964 the
fifth edition was edited by W.F. Bernhardt; it and the
earlier editions are still important reference tools.

1905   The first fifth-year program in library education
is pioneered at Simmons College; a condensed one-year
program is offered to graduates of approved colleges
(White p. 146).

1905   Apprentice classes are set up at the St. Louis
Public Library to train personnel (White p. 148); they
develop into a standard-grade library school by 1917.

1905   The Southern Library School opens at Atlanta,
Georgia (White p. 145); it becomes the Emory School,
see also 1907.

1905   The first lectures on government publications are

added to library education, under James I. Wyer at the Albany School (White p. 99).

1905 A trend toward the modern high school library in the U. S. begins with the appointment this year of full-time librarians for the schools. (EB 1950, v. 14, p. 24).

1905 The main alphabet of the B. M. printed catalog is completed; the first general catalog of a major modern library to be printed in full, cf. +Esdaile, p. 135.

1905 The first durable carbon paper, permitting duplicate copies on the typewriter, appears this year (*Schellenberg p. 83).

1905 The earliest known bookmobile in the U. S. is reported at Washington County Free Library, Hagerstown, Md. (AmLA 1960, p. 179).

1905 The earliest known "package" or mail-order library is reported at the Oregon State Library (ALA-B v. 19, p. 333); the University of Wisconsin is reported to begin a package library service in 1906. AmLA reports university extension service at Oxford as early as 1878, cf. AmLA 1964, p. 201.

1905 The Classification Décimale (CD) is published this year by FID (Tauber p. 199). It began in 1895 as an adaptation of the Dewey Decimal System; in 1927 it was revised and named Classification Décimale Universelle or Universal Decimal Classification (UDC), cf. Dewey, 16th ed.

1905 The Booklist begins with the January issue (AmLA 1958, p. 169). See also 1930.

1905 The Book Review Digest begins publication under H. W. Wilson Company (Lawler p. 164). An abstracting and index service.

1905 The Ames Comprehensive Index to the Publications of the United States Government is published in two volumes by the GPO (Shove p. 105).

1906 The listing of copyright deposits is placed fully under the responsibility of LC (Rogers p. 68); the Catalogue of Title Entries becomes Catalogue of Copyright Entries (the "ue" is dropped in 1934). See also 1891. Major changes are made in the U.S. copyright law this year (see also 1790), and in 1964 other changes will be contemplated, one to repeal the juke-box exemption, cf. LCIB v. 23, no. 23, p. 296, and another to allow computer programs to be registered where elements of literary expression are sufficient and the language is intelligible, cf. LCIB v. 23, no. 20, p. 226.

1906 The American Association of Law Libraries is organized (AmLA 1958, p. 3).

1906 The Society of American Archivists is organized (AmLA 1958, p. 26).

1906 The Antiquarian Booksellers' Association, an international organization, is organized in London (Glaister p. 8).

1906 LC publishes the ALA Portrait Index, now out of print (Shove p. 76).

1906 Otlet and Goldschmidt make the first advances in the micro-photographic book (LibT v. 5, no. 2, p. 277); Vallbehr brings out the earliest known viewer this same year. See also 1939.

1906 The Morrison Check List of American Almanacs, 1639-1800 is published by LC, cf. Drake; a meager listing which is superseded by the Drake Almanacs of the United States in 1962.

1906 The first reported "blurb" appears on a book jacket (Steinberg p. 202). See also item under 1833.

1907 The Yudin Library of Russian Titles is acquired by LC, and foundations are laid for its Orientalia Collection (Mearns p. 184).

1907 The Southern Library School becomes the Library

School of the Carnegie Library, Atlanta; later it becomes the Division of Librarianship, Emory University
(White p. 145). See also 1905.

1907   An endowed reference library opens, the Ann-
mary Brown Memorial Museum at Brown University
(EA Reprint p. 357cc).

1907   The ALA Bulletin begins with the January issue
as the official organ of the American Library Association (AmLA 1958, p. 168).

1907   Chemical Abstracts begins publication (Casey p.
4); under the American Chemical Society.

1907   The Debater's Handbook is published by H.W.
Wilson (Lawler p. 56); from this evolved the Handbook
Series, the Abridged Debater's Handbook, and in 1922
the famous Reference Shelf.

1907   The International Index to Periodicals begins under H.W. Wilson as a supplement to Readers' Guide
(Shove p. 29).

1907   The Cambridge History of English Literature
(CHEL) is published by the Cambridge University Press;
it is reprinted in 1932 (Shove p. 86).

1908   The Anglo-American Code is published (Tauber p.
134); Dewey first proposed the Code in 1904.

1908   The Prussian Instructions are published (Strout
p. 26), considered one of the basic cataloging codes and
still used in some European libraries.

1908   A School of Library Science opens at Syracuse
University, New York (AmLA 1959, p. 179).

1908   The Law Library Journal begins with the January
issue, under the American Association of Law Libraries (AmLA 1959, p. 169).

1908   International copyright: Berlin Convention convenes (Walls p. 62). See item under 1887.

1908 A 3-cutter machine for trimming books is built
by August Fromn in Leipzig (Glaister p. 163). This
is a long way from the "plough" supposedly first used
about 1534 (Blades p. 91); in 1837 Thirault produced the
first paper-cutting machine; in 1844 Mossiquot took out
the first patent on the "guillotine" paper-cutter, cf.
Glaister. The earliest reported folding-machine for
printed sheets was in 1850, in England; the first use in
the U.S. was reported in 1859, cf. Glaister and +Hunt-
er.

1908 A Typographic Library and Museum is founded in
Jersey City by the American Typefounders Company;
Henry L. Bullen, librarian (Brigham p. 129).

1909 The LC printed list of subject headings begins
publication (Tauber p. 161).

1909 The Special Libraries Association is organized
(AmLA 1958, p. 27).

1909 The Pacific Northwest Library Association (PN-
LA) is organized (LibT v. 3, no. 3, p. 322).

1909 The Standard Catalog series begins publication under H.W. Wilson (Lawler p. 68). In 1918 the first
part for public libraries is issued as the "Sociology Section"; in 1928 it appears under title Standard Catalog for
Public Libraries; in 1926-1928 the first Standard Catalog for High School Libraries is issued.

1909 Moody's Manual of Investments begins under
Moody's Investors Service (Shove p. 62).

1910 The LC card copy program begins receiving cataloging done by libraries outside Washington, D.C.
(Tauber p. 123). See also 1902.

1910 The first director of a university library in the
U.S. is reported at Harvard this year (AmLA 1957, p.
126), probably the first major step toward administra-

tion above the management level.   See also 1923.

1910   Special Libraries begins with the January issue, under SLA (AmLA 1958, p. 170).

1910   International copyright: The Buenos Aires Convention convenes (Walls p. 60); open only to Western Hemisphere republics, Canada excluded.

1910   The Guide to Reference Books is edited this year by Mudge (Winchell p. v).   See also 1902; 1941.

1910   The Monthly Checklist of State Publications is first issued, by LC (Schmeckebier p. 76).

1910   The Public Affairs Information Service (PAIS) begins as an SLA project under John A. Lopp (LibJ v. 89, p. 598); its first issue was a mimeographed one in 1913; in 1914 the first issue printed came from H.W. Wilson.

1910   Moulton's Library of Literary Criticism of English and American Authors is published in eight volumes; in 1934 it is reprinted by Peter Smith (Shove p. 87).

1911   Legislation providing county library service is enacted by California, reported a first of its kind in the U.S. (EB 1950, v. 14, p. 24); the state began work with organized county libraries as early as 1909.

1911   A School of Librarianship opens at the University of Washington, Seattle (AmLA 1959, p. 179).

1911   The Bulletin of the Medical Library Association begins publication (AmLA 1958, p. 169).

1911   The American Library Annual begins series I under R.R. Bowker Company (AmLA 1956, Pref.).

1911   The Carnegie Corporation is organized (Predeek p. 108).

1912   An endowed reference library opens, the James

Jerome Hill Reference Library, St. Paul, Minn. (EA Reprint p. 357cc).

1912   The Photostat camera is used in several U.S. libraries--LC, the John Crerar, and the New York Public--as of this date (LibT v. 5, no. 2, p. 270).

1912   A bibliography of American and English annuals is issued by Frederick W. Faxon under title Literary Annuals and Gift Books (Brigham p. 21).   See also 1825.

1912   The Education Directory begins annual publication by the U.S. Office of Education (Shove p. 57).

1913   The earliest known Friends of the Library group is reported at the Bibliothèque Nationale, in this year (SE-Lib. v. 7, no. 3, p. 89).

1913   The 38 Stat. 75 of June 23 places on permanent basis the depositories for U.S. government publications (Schmeckebier p. 109).

1913   The Hawaii Public Library dates from this year (EA 1963, v. 14, p. 5).

1913   The New York Times Index begins its service (Davis p. 328).   An earlier index began in 1851 and came out in three issues, cf. Shove, p. 31.

1913   The Industrial Arts Index begins its service under H.W. Wilson (Shove p. 30); in 1958 it divided into the Applied Science and Technology Index and the Business Periodicals Index.

1914   The first reported library phonodisc collection is found at the St. Paul Public (AmLA 1960, p. 179).   See also 1923.

1914   The Dayton Classes for library education begin at the Dayton Public under Electra Doren; a new method for recruiting for library schools (White p. 159).

1914   A regional union catalog is begun by the California State Library, marked as the first true regional union catalog in the U.S. (Downs p. 7).

1914   The special design for the library building at Johns Hopkins University (Parker, Thomas, Rice, Architects) becomes an influential factor in U.S. library architecture (EB 1950, v. 14, p. 26).

1914   The Wilson Library Bulletin begins with the November issue, under H.W. Wilson (AmLA 1958, p. 176).

1914   The American Institute of Graphic Arts is organized in New York (Glaister p. 6).

1915   The SLA Special Classifications Committee is appointed (AmLA 1965, p. 121); collecting and making available specialized classification schemes begins in 1924; in 1956 the collection is moved to Western Reserve University and housed in the SLA Specialized Classifications Center.

1915   The American Association of School Librarians is organized (AmLA 1958, p. 4).

1915   The Association of American Library Schools is organized (AmLA 1958, p. 14). An ALA Round Table was formed as early as 1907, cf. White, p. 156.

1915   Courses in school-library work are added to the curriculum at Carnegie Tech library school (White p. 148).

1915   LC officially assumes its full role as a Legislative Reference Service (Mearns p. 188). In 1936 it begins issuing the Digest of Public General Bills.

1915   The first reported carrels in U.S. bookstack areas are found at Harvard beginning this year (AmLA 1957, p. 126).

1915   The principle of the Peek-a-boo card is first applied; used in bird identification (Casey p. 125).

1916 The first reported photographic department in a university library is opened this year at Harvard (Am-LA 1957, p. 126). As early as 1877 the Bibliothèque Nationale furnished two darkrooms for patrons' use; in the 1880's the British Museum had photographing facilities for researchers, cf. LibT v. 5, no. 2, p. 267.

1916 Margaret Mann publishes a special subject-headings list for juvenile literature (Tauber p. 164).

1916 The Agricultural Index of H. W. Wilson Company begins publication (Shove p. 73).

1917 The first reported labor unions in U. S. libraries appear, at the New York Public in May, at LC in September (LibQ v. 9, no. 4, p. 492); in 1918 two are reported, at Boston and Washington; in 1919 one is reported at Philadelphia.

1917 Wartime services at home and overseas are begun jointly by ALA and LC (Mearns p. 191).

1917 The Technical Book Review Index begins quarterly publication by the Carnegie Library, Pittsburgh; in 1935 it becomes a project of SLA (Shove p. 66).

1917 The Cambridge History of American Literature (CHAL) begins publication under Putnam; in 1933 it is reprinted by Macmillan (Shove p. 85).

1917 The Biennial Survey of Education begins publication by the U. S. Office of Education; in 1958 it becomes an annual numbered series, under title Statistics of Education in the United States.

1917 The first Pulitzer Prize is awarded in the U. S. (Glaister p. 333).

1918 A guide to cataloging periodicals is produced by LC under the editorship of McNair (ALA 1930, p. 35); in 1919 a guide to cataloging serial publications of societies and institutions is produced, edited by Pierson.

1918   The Census of 15th-Century Books Owned in
America is issued by the Bibliographical Society of
America and the New York Public Library (ALA 1930,
p. 54).   The British Museum Catalogue of Books Printed in the Fifteenth Century was begun in 1908.

1918   Writings on American History for bibliographics,
which began in 1906, begins publication under the GPO
(Shove p. 91).

1918   The Beilstein Handbuch der organischen Chemie
begins publication under Springer, Berlin (Shove p. 69).

1919   The earliest program for young adults (defined by
ALA in 1937 as 13-21 years in age) begins at the New
York Public, with specially trained help (EA 1957, v.
17, p. 356o).

1919   The Henry E. Huntington Library opens at San
Marino, Calif. (EA Reprint p. 357dd).   The trust was
established in 1918.   Its Bulletin begins in 1931, becomes the Quarterly in 1937.

1919   A School of Librarianship opens at the University
of California, Berkeley (AmLA 1959, p. 178).   Predeek
reports that England's first formal training in librarianship begins this year at the University College in London; a two-year course founded under a Carnegie Trust,
cf. Predeek, p. 78.

1919   The first Marshall Field Book Fair is held October 13-18, in Chicago (AmLA 1959, p. 153).

1919   The Hoover Library for War, Revolution and
Peace is founded this year, on the campus of Stanford
University, California, (privately endowed by Herbert
and Lou Henry Hoover) to be a research center with
emphasis on World Wars I and II (American Library
Directory, ed. 24 (1964), p. 104).   See also 1955.

1919   National Children's Book Week is inaugurated in
May at the American Booksellers Association by Franklin K. Mathews, chief librarian for the Boy Scouts of

America (AmLA 1958, p. 189).

1920 The first reported young people's room in a U.S. library is opened at the Cleveland Public (EA 1957, v. 17, p. 356o).

1920 Standards for high school libraries are adopted by NEA and ALA; the first reported in the U.S. (EA 1957, v. 17, p. 356y).

1920 The 3-plus-1 plan for a four-year program in library education is first adopted by Simmons College (White p. 146).

1920 The Southeastern Library Association is organized (LibT v. 3, no. 3, p. 322).

1920 Audio-visual materials begin to appear as a normal part of library service in the U.S. (LibT v. 5, no. 2, p. 295).

1920 Propaganda move: The American Library in Paris opens (EA Reprint p. 349). It was organized in 1918 with Burton Egbert Stevenson as its first librarian.

1920 The Art Index begins its services under the H.W. Wilson Company (Shove p. 76).

1921 The Public Health Engineering Abstracts begins monthly issues under the U.S. Public Health Service (Schmeckebier p. 80).

1921 ALA adopts a standard of a minimum of one dollar per capita for library support (AA 1922, p. 483).

1921 The Nederlands Instituut voor Documentatia en Registratuur (NIDER) is organized to stimulate activity in documentation (Casey p. 576).

1921 The American Merchant Marine Library Association is organized (AmLA 1958, p. 12).

1921 The Catholic Library Association is organized

(AmLA 1958, p. 19).

1921   A Union Catalog of Texas and Southwestern history is begun; earliest known of the subject-restricted catalogs in the U.S. (Downs p. 8).

1921   LC receives custody of the Declaration of Independence and the Constitution (Mearns p. 192). In 1952 both documents, with the papers of the Continental Congress, are placed under custody of the National Archives, cf. AA, 1953, p. 405.

1921   The Bookman's Manual is first published (Hoffman p. vii); it began as a course of lessons, under Bessie Graham, at an evening school in Philadelphia; by the ninth edition in 1960 it had become the Readers' Advisor, edited by Hester R. Hoffman.

1922   The Army Medical Library is the new name given to the Library of the Surgeon General's Office (LibQ v. 28, p. 108).

1922   The Southwest Library Association is organized at the Texas Library Association Conference this year (LibT v. 3, no. 3, p. 322).

1922   The first reported U.S. Friends of the Library: Glen Ellyn, Illinois, and Onondaga County, New York (AmLA 1960, p. 179). A "Friends" group is reported as first appearing at Harvard in 1925, by Powell in the SE-Lib, v. 7, no. 3.

1922   The first Newbery Medal is awarded for the most distinguished contribution to American literature for children (AmLA 1959, p. 115).

1923   A Committee on Classification of Library Personnel is appointed by ALA (Bostwick p. 224), probably the first major step toward a true administration of libraries.

1923   The first reported circulating phonodisc service is begun at Springfield (Mass.) Public Library (AmLA

1960, p. 179). See also 1914.

1923 The Williamson report on training for library service, prepared for the Carnegie Corporation, is issued (White p. 33).

1923 The earliest reported adult education department in a public library is opened at the Milwaukee Public, under Miriam D. Tompkins (LibT v. 1, no. 4, p. 437).

1923 An endowed reference library opens, the Wm. L. Clements Library, Ann Arbor, Michigan (EA Reprint p. 357cc).

1923 The Sears Subject Heading List is published (Tauber p. 163).

1924 An accrediting agency for U.S. library schools is established by ALA in the Board of Education (BEL) (Bryan p. 150). The first proposals for an accrediting agency and standards were made at the Portland Conference in 1905, cf. White, p. 154.

1924 The Pierpont Morgan Library becomes a public reference library (AA 1925, p. 426).

1924 Establishment of the LC musical concert program begins with a grant from the Coolidge Foundation (Mearns p. 195).

1924 Propaganda move: The Paris Library School opens, sponsored by ALA (AA 1925, p. 500).

1924 Contribution to library education: Alexander Meiklejohn's address to ALA concerning the return to the book as the medium for dispensing adult education (Grattan p. 124).

1924 The Association of Special Libraries and Information Bureaux (ASLIB) is organized in London (Predeek p. 62).

1924 The American branch of the Incunabula Society is

145

formed this year (ALA 1930, p. 56); in 1930 it pledges itself to support the Gesamtkatalog.

1924 The Horn Book Magazine begins with the October issue (AmLA 1958, p. 175).

1924 The Logasa and Ver Nooy Index to One-act Plays comes out in its basic volume, under Faxon, Boston (Shove p. 83).

1925 Standards for U.S. library schools are adopted by ALA (White p. 197); proposals for them were first made at the ALA Conference in 1905.

1925 Standards for elementary school libraries are set by NEA and ALA (EA 1957, p. 17, p. 356y).

1925 Julia Pettee publishes a special subject-headings list for theological literature (Tauber p. 164).

1925 The Hampton Institute establishes a library school for Negro librarians (AA 1926, p. 439).

1925 The Gesamtkatalog der Wiegendrucke (GKW) begins in Leipzig (*Carter p. 93); volume 8(F) is begun by 1940.

1926 A Survey of Libraries in the United States, a major library survey, is published in four volumes by ALA (AmLA 1958, p. 114).

1926 The ALA Cooperative Cataloging Committee is appointed (Tauber p. 123). See also 1940.

1926 A Department of Library Science opens at the University of Michigan, Ann Arbor (AmLA 1959, p. 178).

1926 The Albany Library School moves back to Columbia; consists of the Columbia School of Library Service, the New York State Library School, and the New York Public Library School (AA 1927, p. 500).

1926 A survey of adult education in the U.S. is pub-

146

lished by ALA (LibT v. 1, no. 4, p. 439), with funds from the Carnegie Corporation.

1926 Book format: a decision is made that lettering on the spine shall read from bottom to top (Glaister p. 218); this is made by the Publishers' Association, with the Association of Book Sellers, Great Britain; in 1948 they reversed the decision by stating that the lettering should read from top to bottom. Lettering on book spines is thought to have been introduced by Jean Grolier (1479-1565), cf. Glaister, p. 41.

1926 Pollard and Redgrave's A Short-Title Catalogue is published (Glaister p. 375).

1926 Book clubs in the U.S. officially begin with the start of the Literary Guild and the Book-of-the-Month Club this year (Steinberg p. 240). The selection processes of the latter were to be studied in the MS Division of LC, cf. LCIB v. 23, no. 29. For other aspects of U.S. book clubs see Adolf Growoll's American Book Clubs, Dodd, Mead, 1897.

1926 Biological Abstracts begins under auspices of the University of Pennsylvania (Shove p. 70).

1926 The Sears Song Index is published by H.W. Wilson; in 1934 a supplement is brought out (Shove p. 80).

1926 ALA observes its 50th anniversary (AA 1927, p. 439).

1927 A Graduate Library School opens at the University of Chicago (EA 1962, v. 17, p. 398).

1927 An Adult Education Board is appointed at ALA (LibT v. 1, no. 4, p. 358).

1927 New standards for high school libraries are adopted by the Association of Colleges and Secondary Schools (AA 1929, p. 427).

1927 The first successful machine for charging books

is presented by Dickman (Geer p. 21). The earliest known exploratory work was at Gaillard (N.Y.) Public, in 1900.

1927 "Project B" begins at LC, with a Rockefeller grant, a program for a union catalog (ALA 1930, p. 120) and a national bibliography. See also 1956.

1927 The International Library Committee is organized at Edinburgh (EA 1953, v. 17, p. 358).

1927 The Union List of Serials in Libraries of U.S. and Canada (ULS) begins with Gregory as editor (ALA 1930, p. 75). This is the first edition; the second appears in 1943. The first work with serials was in 1859 in the libraries of Milan; in 1876 the Baltimore libraries brought out a work (see 1876); in 1881 the Belgian libraries did the same; in 1885 Bolton edited the Catalog of Science and Technology Periodicals; in 1901 the Chicago Library Club made a list including serial sets; in 1906 this list was expanded by the John Crerar; in 1913 ALA appointed a committee on ULS; in 1959 work begins on the third edition; by 1966 it is completed and published and incorporates all information in the second edition and the supplements of 1945 and 1953, plus selected new titles up to 1950, when NST begins coverage, cf. ULS, ed. 3; LCIB v. 25, no. 5, p. 66.

1927 The Quarterly Cumulative Index Medicus begins publication under the American Medical Association (Beswick p. 62). It grew out of the Index Medicus, see also 1879.

1927 H.G.T. Cannons, Bibliography of Library Economy is brought out by ALA (EB 1950, v. 14, p. 21). The first edition was published in England in 1910; in 1921 a supplement appeared under title Library Literature. See also 1933.

1927 Psychological Abstracts begins under the American Psychological Association (Shove p. 48).

1927   The Firkins Index to Plays is first published by
H. W. Wilson; a supplement appears in 1935 (Shove p.
83).

1927   The first issue of James D. Henderson's News-
Letter of the LXIV MOS appears; a leaflet publication
for the collector of miniature books (Brigham p. 146).

1928   The first PhD in library education is granted at
the University of Chicago Library School (EA 1962, v.
17, p. 398).

1928   Two library schools open: University of Minnesota, Minneapolis; George Peabody College for Teach-
ers, Nashville (AmLA 1959, pp. 178-179).

1928   The public library is defined by a Missouri Court
(Joeckel p. 46); in Carpenter vs St. Louis, the court
declared that the library is an educational enterprise
and a delegated function of the State.

1928   International copyright: Rome Convention convenes (Walls p. 62).   See item under 1887.

1928   A successful photo-composing machine is invented
by Edmund Uher, Hungary; the Uhertype, first called
the Luminotype (Glaister p. 425).   The earliest reported
attempts at photo-composition were by Hunter and August in England in 1922.

1928   Remington Rand obtains the patent for a micro-
camera (Hassert invention) to photograph both sides of
a document (LibT v. 5, no. 2, p. 277); in 1908 Aman-
dus Johnson devised the first microfilm camera.

1928   The Dictionary of American Biography (DAB) begins publication under Scribner (Shove p. 94).

1928   Audio recording on photographic film (the "talk-
ies") becomes commercially practical (Doss p. 193);
work in this field was done all through the 1920's.

1929   The International Federation of Library Associations (IFLA) formulates its statutes at Venice; power is given the International Library Committee (see also 1927) to administer its affairs (EA 1953, v. 17, p. 358).

1929 The earliest reported circulating film library opens at Kalamazoo, Michigan (AmLA 1964, p. 202).

1929 The Rosenwald Fund is established for grants-in-aid to U. S. county libraries (LibT v. 1, no. 4, p. 495). By the 1960's the county libraries, per se, begin to atrophy as State Library extension programs reach the smaller towns.

1929 Two library schools open: Texas Woman's University (College of Industrial Arts; Texas State College for Women), Denton; University of Oklahoma, Norman (AmLA 1959, pp. 178-179).

1929 The Detroit self-charging system is presented at the Detroit Public by Ralph Ulveling (Geer p. 10).

1929 The Education Index begins service from the H. W. Wilson Company (Shove p. 55).

1930 Within this decade the Browsing Room rapidly rose in popularity among U. S. academic institutions, as an innovation to encourage reading for pleasure by the students; some universities had elaborately furnished rooms dedicated to wealthy donors, some had make-shift spaces furnished with castoffs; variations of the idea were campus rental book shops and dormitory-sponsored collections (see also Social Lib. Movement: Student Societies); even some progressive high schools established them.

1930 Dewey classification numbers appear on LC printed cards beginning this year (Tauber p. 192).

1930 The Committee on Code Revision is appointed by ALA (Tauber p. 134).

1930 Federal aid to libraries is granted under a WPA program (LibT v. 1, no. 4, p. 495). Objections are raised in ALA, see also 1935.

1930 Professional librarians are appointed by the Federal Bureau of Prisons to organize prison libraries (EA Reprint p. 357n).

1930 The Inter-American Bibliographers and Librarians Association is organized (AmLA 1958, p. 36).

1930 The E. P. Dutton-John Macrae Award of an annual one thousand dollars is established; it lapses in 1933; is reestablished in 1952 (AmLA 1959, p. 113).

1930 The Subscription Books Bulletin begins publication under ALA (Shove p. 26); in 1956 it combines with the Booklist, see also 1905.

1930 Mott's A History of American Magazines, a bibliography, is published in four volumes, 1930-1957, by Harvard University Press (Shove p. 27).

1930 The Europa and Orbis encyclopedias first appear in looseleaf form (Shove p. 44); in 1960 they appear as the annual Europa Yearbook.

1931 The Pratt-Smoot Act is passed to augment library services to the blind (EA 1957, v. 17, p. 356q); national library services for adult blind are set up at LC and are to be administered by State library agencies.

1931 The ALA Executive Board appoints a committee, under Akers, to study the specialized terminology of librarianship (ALA-G p. iii); in 1941 this committee becomes the Subcommittee on Library Terminology of the ALA Editorial Committee; the first interest in terminology was shown in 1926 by BEL; in 1927 the Elizabeth M. Smith Report was issued; in 1929 BEL appointed a committee under Jennie Flexner to continue the work. See also 1943.

1931 A survey to determine the extent to which conditions of storage are responsible for deterioration of materials is conducted by the U.S. Bureau of Standards

(*Schellenberg p. 161).

1931   The Association of Research Libraries (ARL) is organized (AmLA 1958, p. 17).

1931   The Music Library Association is organized (AmLA 1958, p. 25).

1931   Three Library Schools are opened: Louisiana State University, Baton Rouge; University of North Carolina, Chapel Hill; University of Denver, Colorado (AmLA 1959, p. 178).

1931   The Library Quarterly begins with the January issue from the University of Chicago Press (AmLA 1958, p. 175); editorial work is done in the Library School.

1931   The new building for the Bibliothèque Nationale Suisse at Berne is influential on modern library architecture (EB 1950, v. 14, p. 26).

1931   The National Central Library, London, receives its royal charter; a center for inter-library lending and union catalogues (Predeek p. 72).

1931   The Essay and General Literature Index begins under H.W. Wilson (Lawler p. 166).   See also 1893.

1932   The Folger Shakespeare Library opens in Washington, D.C. (EA 1957, v. 17, p. 357b).

1932   The first reported electrically operated machine charger is introduced by Gaylord (Geer p. 28).

1932   A union catalog is begun by Oregon State Library (Downs p. 362).

1932   The first modular designs for library buildings are introduced by McDonald and Githens (EA 1963, v. 17, p. 393); the designs do not begin to exert real influence until 1945.

1932   The Index Translationum, an international bibliography, is begun by the League of Nations (Glaister p. 201); in 1949 it is continued by Unesco.

1932   The Vertical File Service begins under H. W. Wilson (Lawler p. 167).

1932   The Ulrich's Periodical Directory begins publication (Ulrich p. ix).

1932   The Minerals Yearbook begins publication under the U. S. Bureau of Mines (Shove p. 70).

1932   The smallest book in the world is reported by the Commonwealth Press, Worcester, Mass., after seven years of experimentation; it measures 5/32 x 3/32 inches (Brigham p. 146). Spielmann reports on The Rose Garden of Omar Khayyam, gathered in eight leaves, measuring 3/16 x 1/4 inches; in 1910 Meigs of Cleveland produced an issue of the Rubaiyat of Omar Khayyam measuring 11/32 x 7/32 inches; in 1929-1932 the Kingsport Press, Tenn., produced three volumes of political addresses, each measuring 3/4 x 7/16 inches, type page, from movable type (Spielmann, Introd.).

1933   Public Library Standards is issued by ALA this year (AmLA 1958, p. 114).

1933   A Department of Library Science opens at the University of Kentucky, Lexington (AmLA 1959, p. 178).

1933   Ranganathan publishes his Colon Classification (Tauber p. 210); in 1952 the fourth revised edition appears.

1933   The new building for the Enoch Pratt Library, Baltimore, is an influential factor in U. S. library architecture history (EB 1960, v. 14, p. 26).

1933   Microfilming of newspapers for general purchase is begun by Recordak (LibT v. 5, no. 2, p. 278).

1933   The Kung Library on Gems is acquired by the U. S. Geological Survey Library (EA 1953, v. 17, p. 357t).

1933   The Library Literature indexing service begins
under H.W. Wilson (AmLA 1958, p. 175).   It continues
H.G.T. Cannons', see also 1927.

1933   The Book of the States begins publication under
the Council of State Governments, Chicago (Shove p. 45).

1933   A political censorship of the twentieth century,
the Nazi book burnings in Germany begin this year
(Steinberg p. 218).

1934   A Certification Plan is established by ALA for
the Library Binding Institute, to control book binding
(Feipel p. 21).

1934   A general interest in certification of librarians is
shown in U.S. libraries in 1934 and 1935 (LibJ v. 60,
p. 238).

1934   The "talking book" is added to library service for
the blind (EA 1957, v. 17, p. 356q).   The first voice
of talking books, John Knight, dies in 1964, cf. LCIB
v. 23, p. 297.

1934   The National Historical Publications Commission
is established by act of Congress; it is reconstituted by
the Federal Records Act, 1950 (Hamer p. vii); its purpose is to encourage agencies to preserve and publish
papers important to U.S. history.   In 1961 it publishes
A Guide to Archives and Manuscripts in the United
States.

1934   The U.S. National Archives Act is passed by Congress (EA 1963, v. 2, p. 186).   As early as 1878 Pres.
Hayes recommended such an act in his annual message,
cf. *Schellenberg.

1934   Three union catalogs are begun: New Jersey Public; the Nassau County (N.Y.) Library, and North Carolina State Library (Downs pp. 358; 359; 360).

1934   Serious work with reduced printing to save space
in U.S. libraries begins at this date (LibT v. 5, no. 2,

p. 276). Callimachus is reported to have said, "A big book is a big nuisance"; from his time the cumbrous scrolls were discontinued at the Alexandrian Library and replaced by papyrus rolls of a small convenient size, cf. *Putnam, pp. 141-142. See also item under Microprint, 1939; also 1460; 1500.

1934 The periodical Notes begins with the July issue under the Music Library Association, Music Division of the Library of Congress (AmLA 1958, p. 170).

1934 The United States Government Organization Manual is first published, by GPO; revised annually (Shove p. 45).

1934 The Municipal Year Book begins publication under the International City Managers' Association, Chicago (Shove p. 45).

1935 The Rocky Mountain Region Bibliographic Center for Research is informally organized, the first reported bibliographic center in the world (Downs p. 11). Plans were initiated by Malcolm G. Wyer in the early 1930's; actual work begins this year.

1935 Rules for inter-library loans are drawn up by the International Federation of Library Associations (IFLA) (AmLA 1958, p. 105). Reportedly Henry Swett Green first proposed the cooperative venture to U.S. libraries in 1876.

1935 Federal aid to libraries is endorsed by ALA (EA 1957, v. 17, p. 356a). See also 1930.

1935 An International Library Congress is held at Madrid (EB 1960, v. 14, p. 20).

1935 The Bliss Classification Scheme is published (Tauber p. 208).

1935 A union catalog is begun at Brown University (Downs p. 365).

1935 The Works Project Administration begins programs which produce some invaluable reference tools, from sources never explored before in the U.S., cf. Kull.

1936 ALA sets a standard for 35mm film as best suited for library and research work, at the Richmond Conference (Doss p. 68).

1936 A School of Library Science opens at the University of Southern California, Los Angeles (AmLA 1959, p. 179).

1936 A Library Staff Organizations Round Table is formed at ALA (EA 1953, v. 17, p. 358).

1936 Three union catalogs are begun: Philadelphia Metropolitan area; Cleveland area, and Vanderbilt University (Downs pp. 12; 360; 366).

1936 The first reported punched card charging system is devised by Ralph Parker at the University of Texas (Geer p. 110). A second "automated" circulation system is reported at Montclair, N.J. Public in 1941; Parker does further work at the University of Missouri, cf. Schultheiss.

1936 The Educational Film Guide begins publication under H.W. Wilson (Lawler p. 166).

1937 The World Congress for Documentalists meets in Paris in August (Casey p. 580).

1937 The Theatre Library Association is organized (AmLA 1958, p. 29).

1937 A union catalog is begun for Ohio (Downs p. 361).

1937 The American Documentation Institute is organized (AmLA 1958, p. 5). It grew out of activities in documentation begun in 1926 by Science Service, and in 1935 by Bibliofilm Services of the Department of Agriculture Library, cf. LibT v. 1, no. 2, pp. 192-193.

1937 The American Imprints Inventory is begun under the Historical Records Survey of WPA (McMurtrie p. 353).

1937 The Joseph W. Lippincott Award, an annual certificate plus five hundred dollars, is first made (AmLA 1958, p. 136).

1937 The American Guide Series begins under the Federal Writers' Project, WPA (Shove p. 100).

1938 A Code of Ethics for Librarians is adopted by the ALA Council on December 26 (AmLA 1958, p. 112).

1938 The Library Services Division is established in the U.S. Office of Education (EA 1958, v. 17, p. 357y); in 1958 it is reorganized as Library Services Branch. In 1964 it attains full Division status, with branches of its own, cf. LCIB v. 23, no. 19, p. 219; in 1965 it becomes part of the Bureau of Adult and Vocational Education, Office of Education, cf. LCIB v. 24, no. 29, Appendix II.

1938 The New England Library Association is organized this year (LibT v. 3, no. 3, p. 322).

1938 The Wilson printed card service begins under H. W. Wilson Company (Lawler p. 71).

1938 A Department of Library Science is opened at Catholic University of America, Washington, D.C. (AmLA 1959, p. 178).

1938 Two union catalogs begin, Nebraska and the New Hampshire State Library (Downs p. 357).

1938 Clyde E. Pettus publishes a special subject-headings list for literature in the field of education (Tauber p. 439).

1938 A Committee on Institutional Libraries is appointed by the American Prison Association (EA Reprint p. 357n).

1938   Special postal rates on books become effective in the U.S. (EA 1957, v. 17, p. 356d).   See also 1958.

1938   A Library Unions Round Table is organized at ALA this year (EA 1953, v. 17, p. 358).

1938   The Journal of Documentary Reproduction begins under ALA (LibT v. 5, no. 2, p. 278).   It ceases publication in 1942.

1938   The American Archivist begins with the January issue, under the Society of American Archivists (AmLA 1958, p. 169).

1938   The first Caldecott Medal is awarded for the most distinguished American picture book for children (AmLA 1959, p. 115).

1938   The National Organization for Decent Literature (NODL), a Catholic censorship group, begins in the U.S. (AmLA 1959, p. 94).

1938   University Microfilms begins its publications service (LibT v. 5, no. 2, p. 278).

1938   Xerography, a dry photographic copying, is invented by Chester F. Carlson (Doss p. 105).   The process is developed commercially by 1946, see Glaister p. 449.

1938   The Bibliographic Index begins under H.W. Wilson, a bibliography of bibliography (Shove p. 22).

1938   Dissertation Abstracts begins service this year, under title Microfilm Abstracts (*Altick p. 91); the title change comes in 1951.

1939   The classification and pay plans for public libraries are published by ALA (EA Reprint, p. 357). See also 1923.

1939   A Library Public Relations Council is appointed (AmLA 1958, p. 23).

1939   College and Research Libraries begins with the
December issue, under the Association of College and
Research Libraries (ACRL) (AmLA 1958, p. 169).

1939   Microphotography is added to library education at
the Columbia School of Library Service (LibT v. 5, no.
2, p. 278).

1939   The Census Library Project is inaugurated at
LC this year (Downs p. 369).   It ceases in late 1950's.

1939   Two union catalogs begin: Westchester, N.Y.
area, and the Vermont State Library (Downs pp. 359;
366).

1939   The Annex of the Library of Congress opens
(Mearns p. 206).

1939   The Microprint card and Readex, its reader, are
put into use by Albert Boni (LibT v. 5, no. 2, p. 250).
It is reported that some of the clay tablets of the Chaldeans were found to be only one inch long, with writing
so minute as to require a reading lens; some lenses
and writing tools were found also, cf. *Putnam, pp.
149-150.

1939   The Besterman A World Bibliography of Bibliographies is first published, in two volumes, 1939-1940
(*Besterman v. 1, p. ix); a second edition appears 1947-
1949; a third, 1952-1956; three such bibliographies were
issued in the nineteenth century: 1866, Petzholdt, Bibliotheca Bibliographica; 1883, Vallè, Bibliographie des
Bibliographies; 1897, Stein, Manuel de Bibliographie.
See also 1686.

1939   The Commodity Year Book begins annual publication under the Commodity Research Bureau; during 1943-
1947 its publication is suspended (Shove p. 61).

1940   A Committee on Intellectual Freedom is estab-
lished at ALA; it publishes Newsletter on Intellectual
Freedom (EA 1963, v. 17, p. 417).   It calls its first
Conference in 1951, on "free communications."

1940 An inter-library loan code is issued by ALA (AmLA 1959, p. 64); it is completely revised and enlarged in 1952.

1940 The ALA Cooperative Cataloging Committee is absorbed by LC (Tauber p. 123). See also 1926.

1940 The first reported experiments with photographic charging systems are done by Shaw at Gary (Ind.) Public (Geer p. 35); Remington Rand produces the first commercial photographic charging machines in 1947.

1940 The Pacific Northwest Bibliographic Center is organized (Downs p. 367).

1940 A regional catalog for the Atlanta-Athens area, under the editorship of Colvin, begins (Downs p. 356).

1940 A contribution to library education: Branscomb, Teaching With Books, which initiates new ideas of library usage (EA 1962, v. 17, p. 418).

1940 Standards for bibliography are set by the Committee Z 39 of the American Standards Association with CNLA (Malclès p. 30); for definitions, terms, printers' lettering, etc. Library Research in Progress (no. 14, 1965) reports that Tauber has undertaken an investigation into a study of standards in connection with Committee Z 39.

1940 The second census of incunabula in American libraries is issued by the Bibliographical Society of America, edited by Margaret B. Stillwell, under title Incunabula in American Libraries, a Second Census of Fifteenth-Century Books Owned in the United States, Mexico, and Canada (*Carter p. 187). See also 1918. The third census is to be published in 1964, cf. LCIB v. 24, no. 35, p. 461.

1940 The Theatre Library Association journal Broadside begins publication (AmLA 1960, p. 155). See also 1937.

1940   A Committee on Intellectual Freedom is established at ALA (EA 1963, v. 17, p. 417). It publishes Newsletter on Intellectual Freedom.

1940   Mathematical Reviews begins abstracting service under the American Mathematical Society (Shove p. 67).

1940   Current Biography begins publication under H. W. Wilson (Shove p. 92).

1941   The New England Deposit Library is organized to ease the problem of selective weeding and discard (Tauber p. 129).   See also 1958.

1941   The first reported library service to shut-ins is begun at the Cleveland Public (EA 1957, v. 17, p. 356r); administered from a trust left by Frederick W. Judd; particular attention is given to the handicapped child. By the 1960's bibliotherapy is a whole new facet of library service in the U. S.

1941   A tab-system of charging is first reported by Trinity College Library, Washington, D. C. (Geer p. 97).

1941   A School of Library Service opens at Atlanta University, Georgia (AmLA 1959, p. 178).

1941   Special Libraries Resources begins publication, is completed in four volumes in 1947 (EA 1953, v. 17, p. 357dd).

1941   The Guide to Reference Books is brought out this year by Constance Winchell (Winchell p. v).   See also 1910; 1902.

1941   Beals and Brady The Literature of Adult Education is published for the American Association for Adult Education (LibT v. 1, no. 4, p. 443).

1941   The Union List of Microfilms, a cooperative project, is begun by the Philadelphia Bibliographical Center (ULM p. iv); it was initiated in 1940; the List first appears in 1942.

1942   The printing, in book form, of the LC card catalog is begun by Edwards Brothers of Ann Arbor (Schmeckebier p. 72); it comes out under the title A Catalog of Books Represented by Library of Congress Printed Cards, under the auspices of ARL, and is completed in 1946; in 1947 the title becomes Cumulative Catalog of Library of Congress Printed Cards; in 1949 the title changes to The Library of Congress Author Catalog, to have a cumulation of 24 volumes released under that title in 1953; in 1953 the title changes again, to Library of Congress Catalog--Books: Authors; in 1956 it becomes the National Union Catalog.

1942   The Council of National Library Associations (CNLA) is organized (AmLA 1958, p. 21).

1942   A study of Civil Service in U. S. public libraries is made by Herbert Goldhor this year (LibQ v. 13, no. 3, p. 187).

1942   Propaganda move: the first OWI outpost library is opened, in London, adjoining the American Embassy, in December of this year (EA 1953, v. 17, p. 349).

1942   Propaganda move: The Biblioteca Benjamen Franklin opens in Mexico City, under auspices of ALA and the OWI (EA 1953, v. 17, p. 349).

1942   Standards for medical libraries in hospitals are published by the American College of Surgeons (EA 1957, v. 17, p. 356s).

1942   The Dewey Decimal Classification, fourteenth edition, is published (Tauber p. 190).

1942   The Farmington Plan is inaugurated October 9 (Williams p. 12); a cooperative venture in acquisitions for U. S. libraries, it becomes a project of ARL in 1944. By 1965 it is limited to European countries, Public Law 480 Projects being devised to cover Asian countries.

1942   The International Relations Board is established at ALA (LibJ v. 89, p. 4465); it becomes a standing committee in 1956.

1942   Film lending becomes a normal part of library
service at this date (LibT v. 5, no. 2, p. 295).   In
1947 the Carnegie Corporation makes a grant to ALA
to build lending collections of films, cf. EA 1957, v.
17, p. 356p.   See also 1929.

1942   The Bibliography of Agriculture for international
coverage begins under the U.S. Department of Agriculture Library (National Agricultural Library)   (Shove p.
73).

1942   The Information Bulletin of the Library of Congress begins publication this year (AmLA 1960, p. 162).

1943   Standards for Public Libraries is published by
ALA (AmLA 1957, p. 107).   It amends previous recom-
mendations for minimum expenditures, see also 1921.

1943   The ALA Classification and Pay Plan for academic libraries is published (EA Reprint, p. 357).   See
also 1923.

1943   The Educational Film Library Association is organized (AmLA 1958, p. 22).

1943   The ALA Glossary of Library Terms is published
(ALA-G p. iv); the editorial work was completed in
1942.   See also 1931.

1943   The Quarterly Journal of Current Acquisitions begins as a supplement to the Annual Report of the Librarian of Congress (AmLA 1960, p. 162).   In 1965 it
becomes the Quarterly Journal of the Library of Congress.

1943   The John Cotton Dana Award is first made by
Wilson Library Bulletin (AmLA 1958, p. 22).

1943   The Commission on Freedom of the Press begins
its work this year, with grants from Time, Inc. and
Encyclopaedia Britannica, funds to be administered by

the University of Chicago, under a leadership to include Robert Hutchinson and Robert D. Leigh; set up as a nongovernment organization (CFP p. v).

1944   Standards and objectives for prison libraries are published by American Prison Association and the Committee on Institutional Libraries, with aid from ALA (EA 1957, v. 17, p. 356s).

1944   The Association of Hospital and Institutional Libraries is organized (AmLA 1958, p. 16).

1944   The Cooperative Cataloging Manual is issued by LC (Tauber p. 123).

1944   A U.S. information library (OWI) is opened in Paris (EA 1953, v. 17, p. 350).

1944   A Cooperative Committee of Library Building Plans is organized in December; no longer extant (Asheim p. 77).

1944   M.J. Voight publishes his special subject headings for use in the field of physics (Tauber p. 439).

1944   Microcards are introduced by Fremont Rider at this date (LibT v. 5, no. 2, p. 280). Publication of original material on Microcards begins in the 1950's, cf. Doss, p. 87.

1944   The ASM Review of Metal Literature begins as a program for bibliographic control, launched by the American Society for Metals (Casey p. 248).

1944   The University Presses gain a lasting prestige in the U.S. this year, through a Saturday Review special issue dealing with their work (Miller p. 10).

1944   The Nineteenth Century Readers' Guide to Periodical Literature, 1890-1899, with supplementary indexing 1900-1922, is published in two volumes by H.W. Wilson (Shove p. 29).

1945   The Cooperative Acquisitions Project is begun at
LC (Tauber p. 27).

1945   ALA opens an office in Washington to implement
Federal relations (EA 1957, v. 17, p. 356d).

1945   A U.S. information library (OWI) is opened in the
Philippines (EA 1957, v. 17, p. 346).

1945   Propaganda move: The American Book Center
(ABC) is organized (LibJ v. 70, p. 672), a special
service on the part of U.S. libraries to war-affected
areas.   See also 1948.

1945   Unesco is formally organized (UNESCO p. 7); it
began in theory at CAME in 1942 and is formally ratified in 1946; its intensive public library programs begin in 1952, which see; its own library, for the Secre-
tariat, begins in 1946, when it inherits the library of
the International Institute of Intellectual Cooperation,
League of Nations.

1945   Donald Wing begins a continuation of the Short-
Title Catalogue, published by Columbia University Press,
1945-1951 (Glaister p. 375).

1945   A serious study of the cumulative effect of printed matter on the human eye is made in the U.S. by
Luckiesh, under title Reading as a Visual Task (Glaister p. 217).   See also 1957.

1946   An endowed reference library opens, the Linda
Hall Library in Kansas City, Mo. (EA Reprint p. 357cc).

1946   The Documents Expediting Project, a government
documents exchange venture, is organized; participants
are ALA, SLA, ARL, and AALL (Schmeckebier p. 116).

1946   The Jewish Librarians Association is organized
(AmLA 1958, p. 23).

1946   A mechanical retrieval program of mechanized
search procedures is studied at the U.S. Patent Office

(Casey p. 268).

1946   Experimentation with punched cards in a retrieval program is begun by the American Chemical Society (LibT v. 1, no. 2, p. 216).

1946   The first reported attempts at machine translation from one language to another are made by Andrew Booth, in the U.S. (Booth p. 1).

1946   The American Book Publishers Council, Inc. is organized as a non-profit corporation (Glaister p. 6).

1947   A Joint Committee on Library Work as a Career is appointed by ALA (AmLA 1957, p. 41).

1947   The American Theological Library Association is organized (AmLA 1958, p. 13).

1947   A Library School is opened at Florida State University, Tallahassee (AmLA 1959, p. 178).

1947   A full course in Publishing Procedures is inaugurated at Radcliffe College (AmLA 1960, p. 190).

1947   The IBM Corporation demonstrates its Circulation Control System for book charging, at the ALA Conference in San Francisco this year (Geer p. 61).

1947   Booth and Britten introduce the auto-digital calculator for use in machine translation (Booth p. 1). The first auto-digital computer was reported in 1944, cf. Greenberger, p. v.

1947   The Great Books Foundation expands its services to include a free adult education program; discussion groups begin in U.S. public libraries (BB 1948, p. 264). Great Books of the Western World is published in 1952 (EB 1960, v. 18, p. 75).

1947   The United Nations Yearbook begins publication under Columbia University Press (Shove p. 44).

1947 The Brigham History and Bibliography of American Newspapers is first published in book form by the American Antiquarian Society (Shove p. 30); a reprint with a supplement is issued in 1962. The work was begun in 1913 and printed in parts in the Proceedings of the Society.

1948 The Library Bill of Rights is adopted by ALA Council on June 18 (AmLA 1958, p. 113). It is revised in 1961.

1948 A conference on special training for librarians is held by the CNLA Sub-Committee on Special Library Education at Princeton University (Bryan p. 326).

1948 ALA ceases accreditation of library school programs until further studies are made (Bryan p. 326).

1948 The Mountain-Plains Library Association is founded (LibT v. 3, no. 3, p. 322).

1948 A National Plan for Public Library Service, standards, is published by ALA (EA 1957, v. 17, p. 356c). The Post-War Standards for Public Libraries, a preliminary statement, was published in 1943.

1948 The USIS (OWI) libraries are established by the Smith-Mundt Act this year (AA 1949, p. 390). These libraries, which began in OWI, moved to the State Department in 1945, and have now come under the general information program, United States Information Service (USIS); in 1953 they become part of the United States Information Agency (USIA). See also 1942; 1944; 1945. In the mid-1960's conditions abroad cause the closing of some of these libraries.

1948 The Wayne County (Mich.) Charging System is put into effect this year (Geer p. 75).

1948 The first reported use of an audio charging system is made at St. Louis County (Mo.) Public (Geer p. 54).

1948   The Vatican rules for the cataloging of printed
books are printed in English; considered one of the basic codes (Strout p. 26).   The rules were first published
in Latin in 1931 (Pettee p. 135).

1948   A Graduate School of Library Science is opened
at the University of Texas, Austin (AmLA 1959, p. 179).

1948   Phono-records become part of library service materials this year (LibT v. 5, no. 2, p. 296).

1948   The U. S. Book Exchange (USBE) is established
(AmLA 1958, p. 29).   It assumes the commitments of
ABC (see 1945), which ceases operation in June of this
year, with a grant from the Rockefeller Foundation and
contracts with the U. S. Department of State and the
Marshall Plan; in 1959 the grant terminates, fees are
paid by the participants, and the Exchange becomes self-
supporting.

1948   The Filmstrip Guide begins publication under
H. W. Wilson (Lawler p. 167).

1948   The International Council on Archives is organized (AmLA 1958, p. 37).

1948   Beta Phi Mu, international library science honor-
ary fraternity, is organized at the University of Illinois
(AmLA 1958, p. 202).

1948   The Booth and Richen dictionary, to be used in
machine translation, is presented (Booth p. 1).

1948   International copyright: Brussels Convention convenes (Walls p. 62).   See also item under 1887.

1948   The Contura is first used, making possible the
copying of an open book, by F. G. Ludwig at Columbia
(LibT v. 5, no. 2, p. 273).

1948   The International League of Antiquarian Booksellers is organized (*Carter p. 119); known as ILAB or
Ligue Internationale de la Librairie Ancienne (LILA).

1948   The Rotofoto of George Westover, London, is
first used; early form of photo-setting machine (Glaister p. 358).

1948   An international handbook on educational exchange,
Study Abroad, begins publication under Unesco (Shove p.
56).

1948   The Demographic Yearbook begins publication under the United Nations (Shove p. 63).

1948   Nuclear Science Abstracts begins service under
the auspices of the U.S. Atomic Energy Agency (Shove
p. 68).

1948   The Biography Index begins its service under the
H.W. Wilson Company (Shove p. 92).

1948   Books in Print (BIP) begins publication under
R.R. Bowker (Shove p. 24).

1949   The Public Library Inquiry, a major library survey, begins under the general editorship of Robert D.
Leigh, for the Social Science Research Council (AmLA
1958, p. 114).   It appears in the following works
(starred titles are reports to the Council):   *Michigan
University Survey Research Center, The Public Library
and the People, 1948; Berelson, The Library's Public,
1949; Garceau, The Public Library in the Political Process, 1949; *Klapper, The Effects of Mass Media, 1949;
*Luening, Music Materials and the Public Library, 1949;
McCamy, Government Publications for the Citizen, 1949;
Miller, The Book Industry, 1949; *Pierce, Work Measurement in Public Libraries, 1949; Waldron, The Information Film, 1949; Campbell, Public Use of the Library and Other Sources of Information, 1950; Leigh,
The Public Library in the United States (the general report), 1950; *Armstrong, Money For Libraries, 1951;
Bryan, The Public Librarian, 1952.

1949   Rules for standard cataloging are issued in two
separate works: The rules for descriptive cataloging are
issued by LC and the rules for main entry are issued

by ALA (Tauber p. 135). Preliminary editions appeared in 1941 and 1947.

1949 A certification program for medical librarians is inaugurated by the Medical Library Association (EA 1957, v. 17, p. 356s).

1949 The first reported separate Undergraduate Library in the U.S. opens at Harvard (AmLA 1957, p. 126).

1949 The Indiana University Division of Library Science opens at Bloomington (AmLA 1959, p. 178).

1949 The first reported library with its own broadcasting permit is Louisville (Ky.) Public, with a 10-watt radio station, sending six hours daily of educational programs (UBL v. 11, no.6, p. 206). The earliest experiments with transmitting sound are reported to be by Hooke, in 1667, using a taut string; the use of "sound" has not been fully exploited by library services, but radio and TV have both been used to some extent in educational programs and public relations promotional work; an audio charge system is reported in 1948.

1949 Propaganda move: International Youth Library established at Munich, Germany, under the auspices of ALA and the Rockefeller Foundation (AA 1953, p. 403).

1949 RCA experiments with the facsimile hand scanner, a step toward the mechanization of bibliographic control (Casey p. 560). The cathode-ray tube was first used in 1895; the first photo sent by wire in 1922; the iconoscope and kinescope first used in 1923, cf. Fabre, "Chronology." See also 1951.

1949 The Unesco Book-token Scheme is launched with thirteen member states, and 150 thousand dollars in coupons to purchase books, periodicals, or photo-copies of educational, scientific, or cultural materials; its purpose is to overcome the barriers of national currencies, import duties, etc. It was first proposed in 1947; ALA endorses it in 1952, cf. UBL v. 17, no. 4, pp. 203-214.

1949   The Margaret Mann Citation is established; the first annual award is given in 1950 (AmLA 1959, p. 155).

1949   The Antiquarian Booksellers' Association of America is organized (*Carter p. 23).

1949   The Frankfort Fair reopens (Glaister p. 147). See also 1473.

1949   Studies in Bibliography begins publication (AmLA 1960, p. 162), the Papers of the Bibliographical Society of the University of Virginia.

1949   Education Abstracts begins as a quarterly under Unesco (Shove p. 55).

1949   The Statistical Yearbook of the UN Statistical Office begins publication this year (Shove p. 63).

1950   The LC printed catalog starts in January to issue its Library of Congress Catalog--Books: Subjects (Schmeckebier p. 72).

1950   A Library Manual for Correctional Institutions is published (EA 1957, v. 17, p. 356s).

1950   The Thermofax, for photo-reproduction, is devised by the makers of Scotch Tape (LibT v. 5, no. 2, p. 283).

1950   Library Science Abstracts begins service under the Library Association of Great Britain (Glaister p. 230); in 1956 a second series begins.

1950   The first reported use of a closed telegraphic system for inter-library lending: a Teletypwriter Exchange System (TWX) from Milwaukee to Racine (LibT v. 5, no. 2, p. 210).

1950   This decade sees great advances in the use of computerized processes and automation for essential library services: text transcription, indexing and abstracting, document selection, information processing, systems for information retrieval, circulation of materials, many technical processes in order work, cataloging, handling of serials publication, etc. The most ambitious programs are those of Parker at the University of Missouri, cf. Casey; Doss; Schultheiss; Sharp; LADP.

1950   Alpha Beta Alpha, national undergraduate library science fraternity, begins at Northwestern State College of Louisiana on May 3 (AmLA 1959, p. 179).

1950   An index to Short-title Catalogue is published; prepared by Paul G. Morrison under the University of Virginia Bibliographical Society (Glaister p. 375).

1950   The British National Bibliography (BNB) begins in January, under the Council of the British National Bibliography, London (Glaister p. 47). The British Catalogue of Music begins in 1957 (Shove p. 25).

1950   The United Nations Documents Index is begun by the Library of the United Nations (Shove p. 107).

1950   Malclès, Les Sources du Travail Bibliographique begins publication in three parts from 1950-1958 (Shove p. 22); an extensive guide to reference materials.

1951   Successful rotary printing from photocomposition becomes possible this year (Glaister p. 112). Photoset and etched magnesium plates successfully combine for indirect rotary printing, under Intertype Fotosetter, in the U.S.

1951   Standards for accrediting U.S. library schools are adopted by the ALA Council on July 13 (AmLA 1961, p. 213).

1951   The Dewey Decimal Classification, fifteenth edition, is published (Tauber p. 190). Known as the "Standard" edition, it does not include "Relative Index" in the title.

1951   The Midwest Inter-Library Center (MILC) is established (Tauber p. 129). In 1965 it becomes the Center for Research Libraries (CRL), cf. LCIB v. 24, no. 12, pp. 144-145.

1951 The Double Call Slip charging system is presented by Parker at the University of Missouri (Geer p. 140).

1951 A survey of recruitment programs is conducted by the Committee on Recruiting and Personnel of the Association of American Library Schools (LibQ v. 27, no. 4, p. 307).

1951 The Coordinate Indexing System is published by Mortimer Taube (LibT v. 1, no. 2, p. 223).

1951 The first successful Remote Facsimile Duplicator is reported by RCA for the Atomic Energy Commission (LibT v. 5, no. 2, p. 212). See also 1949.

1951 Propaganda move: a Japanese library school is established at Keio University, sponsored by the U.S. Army of Occupation and administered by ALA (AA 1952, p. 416).

1951 A Fund for Adult Education is established by ALA (EA 1957, v. 17, p. 356p).

1951 The American Heritage Project begins, sponsored by the Fund for Adult Education (EA 1957, v. 17, p.356p).

1951 The International Association of Music Libraries (IAML) is organized at Paris under the auspices of Unesco (Currall p. 1); it was first proposed in 1949, at Florence; receives its constitution in 1952.

1951 The Hampshire Interlibrary Center is founded at the University of Massachusetts (Am. Library Directory, ed. 24 (1964), p. 397); it proposes to purchase and store jointly owned research materials for Mount Holyoke, Smith, Amherst, University of Massachusetts, Forbes Library, Northampton, Mass.

1951 The New Serials Titles (NST) begins publication

(Schmeckebier p. 73). It begins coverage with 1950.

1951   A printed book catalog is reported done by computerized processes at King County (Wash.) Public this year (Schultheiss p. 5); another is reported for the Los Angeles Public in 1956.

1951   The CARE children's book fund is established in February of this year (AmLA 1961, p. 65).

1951   The Hans Christian Andersen Medal is established by the International Board on Books for Young People (Glaister p. 175).

1951   ALA observes its 75th anniversary (AA 1952, p. 27).

1951   A Conference on Rural Reading is called by the U.S. Department of Agriculture (AmLA 1957, p. 169).

1952   The Armed Forces Medical Library is the new name for the Army Medical Library (EA 1957, v. 17, p. 357k).

1952   A survey of adult education activities in U.S. public libraries is conducted by ALA (AA 1953, p. 27).

1952   The first Unesco pilot library for public library service is established, in Delhi, India (AA 1953, p. 728). In 1954 a second one is opened at Medellèn, Columbia; in 1958 a third at Enugu, Eastern Nigeria; in 1962 a fourth one is projected for the Ivory Coast, Africa.

1952   Studies in techniques of machine retrieval are held at MIT (LibT v. 1, no. 2, p. 216).

1952   A conference on machine translation is held at MIT (Booth p. 2); it continues the work begun by Booth and Britten.

1952   The first experiments with industrial TV in a library are reported at LC; a program for reference and verification (LibT v. 5, no. 2, p. 209).

174

1952 Standards for Library School Programs in Teacher Education is issued by ALA Committee on Accreditation (ALA-B v. 52, no. 9, p. 695).

1952 The Ranganathan catalog code, third edition, is published; it is an influence on U.S. codes (Strout p. 26).

1952 Public relations: U.S. public libraries cooperate with the National Non-Partisan Register and Vote Campaign in a program to increase the number of informed voters, sponsored by the American Heritage Foundation, ALA and others (AA 1953, p. 404).

1952 The Universal Copyright Convention (UCC) convenes; Unesco and 36 countries (Glaister p. 426). Not to be confused with the Berne or the Pan-Am conventions, cf. Walls.

1952 The Melvil Dewey Medal is established by Forrest Press as an annual award; first given in 1953 (AmLA 1959, p. 113).

1952 The Verifax is devised to reduce the expense of duplication processes (LibT v. 5, no. 2, p. 275).

1952 Solid Dot Braille is devised, an alternative to regular Braille writing (Glaister p. 45).

1952 The ACRL Monographs begin with the January issue (AmLA 1958, p. 168).

1952 School Libraries begins with the fall issue (AA 1953, p. 404).

1952 Library Trends begins with the July issue, from the University of Illinois Library School (AmLA 1958, p. 175).

1953 Reading improvement programs begin at Providence (R.I.) Public (AmLA 1958, p. 198); others begin at Brooklyn Public in 1955.

1953   A manual of photo-reproduction is published by
FID; for document reproduction through photocopy, and
techniques and equipment in photocopying (LibT v. 5,
no. 2, p. 267).

1953   The Public Relations Planner is issued; moderate-
ly priced public relations and cooperation services for
libraries (EA 1957, v. 17, p. 356).

1953   The Freedom to Read Statement is issued by ALA
(AA 1954, p. 410).

1953   The Rutgers Graduate School of Library Service
opens at Rutgers University, New Brunswick, N.J.
(AmLA 1959, p. 179).   Schools accredited since 1959 are
at Rosary College, State University of New York, UCLA,
University of Pittsburgh, Western Michigan, Western Reserve, cf. AmLA 1966.

1953   The Customs Simplification Act, concerning printed and educational matter, is passed (Tauber p. 52).

1953   The Photoclerk is demonstrated by the American
Council of Learned Societies; a Remington Rand product
(LibT v. 5, no. 2, p. 276).

1953   The National Library of Canada at Ottawa opens
this year (Esdaile p. 310).

1953   The Theological Library Association journal Newsletter begins this year (AmLA 1960, p. 154).   See also
1947.

1953   A national conference for volunteers working with
books for the blind convenes this year (AA 1954, p. 410).

1953   The Grolier Society Award, an annual plaque plus
$500, is established (AmLA 1959, p. 112).

1954   The LC printed catalog issues two new sections:
one for motion pictures and filmstrips, another for music and phonorecords (Schmeckebier p. 75).

1954 The LC service-to-the-blind program is extended to include children (EA 1959, v. 17, p. 408).

1954 Beginning this year all Federal libraries, except LC, are placed under Civil Service (EA 1957, v. 17, p. 356f).

1954 As of this date 45 states have voluntary or mandatory certification laws of some type (EA 1957, v. 17, p. 356f). A report on certification by public libraries in the U.S. is made by the ALA Certification Committee under LAD in 1958.

1954 Documentation is defined by DGD for FID (Casey p. 576); "To conduct documentation means, in a systematic fashion, to bring together documents, to analyze them, and to render them useful. This activity is documentation. "

1954 Propaganda move: The American Memorial Library is established in Berlin (LCIB v. 23, no. 20, p. 225).

1954 The Osteopathic Library Association is organized (AmLA 1958, p. 26).

1954 Aided by RCA, LC experiments with the facsimile scanner for long-distance sending of images (Casey p. 559). See also 1949; 1951.

1954 The Microlex card is devised, capable of holding 200 pages of text (LibT v. 5, no. 2, p. 280).

1954 Machine translation experiments are continued at Georgetown University, with IBM; the periodical M.T. appears (Booth p. 4).

1954 The U.S. Senate ratifies UCC on June 25 (AmLA 1956, pp. 100-101); certain laws still had to be brought into accord; instruments of ratification are deposited in August, thus ending 70 years of effort to bring U.S. copyright laws into workable relations with the rest of the world.

1954   The ACRL Microcard Series begins publication
(Tauber p. 402).

1954   The National Book Committee is organized
(AmLA 1958, p. 191) by ALA and the American Book Publishers Council.

1954   The Beta Phi Mu Award, a citation plus $50, is
established (AmLA 1959, p. 112).

1954   The Electrofax, a photoduplication machine, is
produced by RCA (LibT v. 5, no. 2, p. 284).

1954   This year sees the beginning of a ban on the com-
ic book (AmLA 1956, p. 94).

1955   A survey on use of TV in public libraries is conducted by the PLD Reporter (AmLA 1958, p. 198).

1955   A Committee on Censorship is appointed by ALA
(AmLA 1959, p. 94).

1955   The Library-Community Project begins, through
the Fund for Adult Education (AA 1957, p. 30).   See
also 1956.

1955   An International Library Congress convenes at
Brussels (EB 1960, v. 14, p. 20).

1955   The Foreign Newspaper Microfilm Project begins
under ARL (Asheim p. 83).

1955   Machine translation experiments are continued at
Birkbeck College, University of London, using the M 2
computer (Booth p. 2).   See also 1952; 1946.

1955   The International Association of Agricultural Librarians and Documentalists is organized (AmLA 1958,
p. 36).

1955   The Universal Copyright Convention is formally
ratified (AmLA 1956, pp. 100-101); it is to go into effect three months after ratification by the twelfth nation;

Monaco fulfills the terms by ratifying on June 16; UCC becomes effective on September 16.

1955 Propaganda move: Books for Asian Students, a program initiated by the Asia Foundation (AmLA 1960, p. 66).

1955 The Presidential Libraries Act is passed this year (Schmeckebier p. 325). Since the administration of F.D. Roosevelt the libraries and papers of each president have been placed in a privately endowed reference library, under the General Services Administration; the Roosevelt was established by joint resolution of Congress, 1939, at Hyde Park; the Truman, 1957, at Independence, Mo.; the Eisenhower, 1960, at Gettysburg; the Kennedy is being subscribed for Harvard (1966); the Johnson is established, 1965, at the University of Texas, Austin. The Hoover Foundation plans (1960) a library museum for the Herbert Hoover private papers, etc., at West Branch, Iowa. Cf. Schmeckebier. Two other memorial collections in honor of presidents are the Hayes Memorial Library, Ohio, and the Harding Memorial.

1955 A Conference on American Books Abroad is convened in September by the National Book Committee, with a grant from the Rockefeller Fund (AmLA 1960, p. 64). A second conference convenes in 1957, resulting in an export guide, Books from the U.S.A., a bi-monthly published by R.R. Bowker.

1955 The Blanck Bibliography of American Literature, part one, is published (Brigham p. 62).

1955 Current National Bibliographies is brought out by LC (Schmeckebier p. 75).

1955 Paperbound Books in Print begins as a quarterly guide under R.R. Bowker (Shove p. 25).

1956 The LC printed catalog becomes the National Union Catalog (AmLA 1961, p. 98). See also 1927; 1942.

1956 The Library Services Act becomes effective June 6 (AmLA 1958, p. 117); a Federal grant-in-aid program for State library extension programs. Cf. AmLA, and LCIB, passim, for progressive changes in the Act.

1956 Public Library Service: A Guide to Evaluation, a new statement of public library standards, is approved by the ALA Council in June (AmLA 1958, p. 114).

1956 A survey of reference services in U.S. public libraries is made by ALA, is published in 1961 (LibT v. 12, no. 3, p. 376); regional reference service for the U.S. had been proposed as early as 1898, at an ALA Conference, by Charles Davidson.

1956 The Joint Library Committee on Copyright is appointed by ARL (LibJ v. 90, p. 3403); surveys library practices with respect to photocopying; joins with SLA Committee in 1957.

1956 The Council on Library Resources is organized in September, with a grant from the Ford Foundation (AmLA 1958, p. 136).

1956 The Library-Community Project: four pilot libraries for adult education programs are established (AA 1957, p. 30); in Kansas, Maryland, Michigan, Tennessee.

1956 The American Library Annual begins Series II under R.R. Bowker (AmLA 1956, Pref.).

1956 Propaganda move: Legislation is enacted by Congress to permit use of foreign currencies accruing under the Agriculture Trade Development and Assistance Act to finance translations of textbooks in 29 countries (AmLA 1961, p. 64).

1956 The Council on Documentation Research is organised (AmLA 1958, p. 21).

1956 The National Library of Medicine is established in the U.S. (AmLA 1959, p. 78). It began in the Surgeon General's Office Library, see 1836; 1922; 1952.

1957 A recruitment program for potential librarians is established by ALA (AmLA 1960, p. 176).

1957 Public Law 85-147 authorizes LC to arrange, index, and microfilm the papers of the 23 U.S. presidents represented in LC holdings (AmLA 1959, p. 75). The Public Papers of the Presidents of the United States begins 1958, with Eisenhower; it is recommended by the National Historical Publication Commission that the papers be issued annually, each volume to cover a calendar year (Schmeckebier p. 317). Since the administration of F.D. Roosevelt, the libraries and papers of each president have been placed in a privately endowed reference library, see 1955.

1957 The Air Pollution Bibliography, compiled by TID for the Public Health Service, is first published this year by LC (Schmeckebier p. 75); a second issue appears in 1959; it began as Bulletin 537 of the U.S. Bureau of Mines.

1957 Library Resources and Technical Services, a journal for catalogers and classifiers, begins publication (AmLA 1960, p. 155).

1957 Selective government document deposit is established by U.S. law (70 Stat. 369) making permanent a former ruling (Schmeckebier p. 113). By 1965 regional depositories are established for complete holdings of all government publications.

1957 The order routines at the University of Missouri are set up on computers this year (Schultheiss p. 4).

1957 A pilot searching-service using machines for bibliographic control is launched by ASM; a file of encoded abstracts is scanned (Casey p. 248). See also 1955.

1957 The Exhibits Round Table Award is established, a $500 annual award by ALA (AmLA 1959, p. 112).

1957   The Liberty and Justice Book Awards are established, three awards of $5,000 by ALA (AmLA 1959,
p. 112).

1957   Propaganda move: American Panorama is distributed through the Carnegie Corporation (AmLA 1958,
p. 98).   A collection of 350 American books given to
250 libraries in 28 different countries, cf. LibJ for
Sept. 15, 1957.

1957   Propaganda move: a 2,000-volume technical library is given to Ghana by the U.S. as an independence
gift (AmLA 1960, p. 65).

1957   The cumulative effect of printed matter on the
human eye is studied by Burt, of London, under title
A Psychological Study of Typography (Glaister p. 217).
See also 1945.

1957   The BIP Subject Guide begins publication (Shove
p. 25).   See also 1948.

1957   The Air Pollution Bibliography begins at LC
(Schmeckebier p. 75).

1957   The Library of Congress publishes the third edition of the union catalog service, Newspapers on Microfilm (*Altick p. 77); a fourth edition is issued in 1961.

1958   The LC printed catalog adds a section on U.S.
manuscript collections: National Union Catalog of Manuscript Collections (AmLA 1961, p. 68); funds furnished
by CLR.

1958   The Lubetzky rules for a cataloging code are presented (Eaton p. 21).   These rules are revised in 1960;
his Critique appeared in 1955.

1958   Studies in compact storage and selective book retirement are held by Yale University and others at a
Washington meeting (LCIB v. 22, no. 48, p. 642).   This is
an attempt to solve the inherent problem of libraries:
to make everything available, even the little-used. See

also 1887; 1941.

1958 A loan service of films captioned for the deaf be-
gins on September 2 of this year (AmLA 1960, p. 108);
Public Law 85-905 provides this service through the
U.S. Department HEW.

1958 The Standards for Undergraduate Library Science
Programs is issued by the ALA Committee on Accreditation (ALA-B v. 52, p. 695).

1958 New postal rates on books go into effect in the
U.S. on August 1 (AmLA 1960, p. 126). See also 1938.

1958 The motion picture preservation program begins
at LC (LCIB v. 23, no. 1, p. 16). See also item under 1894.

1958 A full size book by photo-reproduction is made
possible by University Microfilms (AmLA 1959, p. 99);
it begins a service at three cents per page. See also
1844.

1958 Censorship: The Citizens for Decent Literature
is organized at Cincinnati (AmLA 1961, p. 132); an
extra-legal group operating at local, state and national
levels.

1958 A Graduate Institute of Book Publishing is established at New York University (AmLA 1960, p. 190).

1958 Pamphlet size is set at 49 pages by a Unesco
standard (LibT v. 10, no. 2, p. 249). To the librarian
the pamphlet is a nuisance, both in housing and statistics; he would not appreciate Orwell's backward look to
the days of pamphleteering and his hope for a return to
this format! Cf. Bernard Bailyn's Pamphlets of the
American Revolution, Vol. I, Harvard University Press,
1965.

1958 National Library Week is established by ALA and
the National Book Committee (AmLA 1959, p. 160).

1958   The Aurxanne Award is established (AmLA 1959, p. 112); a $200 award for the best children's book about animals.

1958   The American Bibliography, 1801-1819 begins publication (Shaw p. ix), edited by Shaw and Shoemaker, to fill the gap in our national bibliography.

1958   Two periodical indexes begin this year, Applied Science and Technology and Business Periodicals under H.W. Wilson (Shove p. 66). See also 1913.

1959   Standards for college libraries are issued, approved by ACRL and ALA (AmLA 1961, p. 123).

1959   The first LC cards printed in Oriental languages are issued (AmLA 1961, p. 68); Chinese, Japanese and Korean materials are prepared by photo-composing machines, using printing rather than calligraphy.

1959   The Library Technology Project (LTP) is established at ALA on May 1 (AmLA 1960, p. 100). It is co-sponsored by the Council on Library Resources; in 1964 the Office for Research is founded.

1959   The second Cataloging-in-source experiment is launched (USLC p. xviii); funds furnished by CLR. See also 1879.

1959   The Dewey Decimal Classification, sixteenth edition, is published (Tauber p. 190).

1959   A service program begins for handicapped and exceptional children, Cincinnati Public (LibT v. 12, no. 1, p. 65); the first reported service for the latter.

1959   The U.N. accepts the gift of the Ford Foundation for a permanent building for its library (DHL p. 27). The Library began in San Francisco in 1945; in 1946 it moved to Lake Success; in 1950 the Woodrow Wilson Foundation presented it with a collection of documents on the League of Nations, the Foundation, and other peace movements, and the Library moved to New York;

in 1961 it is dedicated as the Dag Hammarskjöld Library, a memorial to the late Secretary General.

1959   Library Research in Progress begins publication, with John C. Rather as editor (AmLA 1961, p. 194).

1959   The Costs of Public Library Service begins as a supplement to Public Library Service (AmLA 1961, p. 114); an ALA project, see also 1956.

1959   Translators and Translations, services and sources compiled by Frances Kaiser for SLA, is published this year (CBI).

1959   The United States Code, 1958 edition, is published by GPO, in 13 volumes (Shove p. 59).   The first codification of Federal laws appeared in 1877 under title Revised Statutes; the second codification was the United States Code, first edition in 1926.

Abbreviations

AALL	American Association of Law Libraries
AALS	Association of American Library Schools
AASL	American Association of School Librarians
ABC	American Book Center
	American Book-Prices Current
ACRL	Association of College and Research Libraries
AEC	Atomic Energy Commission
ALA	American Library Association
ARL	Association of Research Libraries
ASLIB	Association of Special Libraries and Information Bureaux
ASM	American Society for Metals
BAR	Book Auction Records
BEL	Board of Education for Librarians
BIP	Books in Print
BLS	Bachelor of Library Science
B. M.	British Museum
BNB	British National Bibliography
CAB	Civil Aeronautics Board
CAME	Conference of Allied Ministers of Education
CARE	Cooperative for American Remittances to Europe
CBEL	Cambridge Bibliography of English Literature
CBI	Cumulative Book Index
CD	Classification Decimale
CFR	Code of Federal Register
CHAL	Cambridge History of American Literature
CHEL	Cambridge History of English Literature
CLR	Council Library Resources
CRL	Center for Research Libraries
CNLA	Council of National Library Associations
DAB	Dictionary of American Biography
DC	Dewey Classification
DGD	Deutsche Gesellschaft für Documentatia
DLS	Doctor of Library Science
DNB	Dictionary of National Biography

EI	Engineering Index
FAA	Federal Aviation Agency
FCC	Federal Communications Commission
FID	Federation Internationale du Documentation (Internation Federation for Documentation)
FPC	Federal Power Commission
FR	Federal Register
FRS	Federal Reserve System
GKW	Gesamtkatalog der Wiegendrucke
GPO	Government Printing Office
GSA	General Services Administration
GW	see GKW
HEW	Health, Education & Welfare
HMSO	Her Majesty's Stationery Office
IAEA	International Atomic Energy Agency
IAI	Industrial Arts Index
ICC	Interstate Commerce Commission
IFLA	International Federation of Library Associations
ILAB	International League of Antiquarian Book-sellers
KWIC	Key word in context
LAD	Library Administration Division
LC	Library of Congress
LIAB	Ligue Internationale de la Librairie Ancienne
LJ	Library Journal
LTP	Library Technology Project
MEDLARS	Medical Literature Analysis & Retrieval Systems
MILC	Midwest Inter-library Center
MIT	Mass. Institute of Technology
MLA	Medical Library Association
	Music Library Association
	Modern Languages Association
MLS	Master of Library Science
MSS	Manuscripts
M. T.	Machine Translation
NAL	National Agricultural Library
NASA	National Aeronautic & Space Administration
NEA	National Education Association
NED	New English Dictionary
NIDER	Nederlands Instituut voor Documentatia en Registratuur

NLM	National Library of Medicine
NODL	National Organization for Decent Literature
NUC	National Union Catalog
NYPL	New York (City) Public Library
NSF	National Science Foundation
NST	New Serials Titles
OED	Oxford English Dictionary
OTS	Office of Technical Services
OWI	Office of War Information
PAIS	Public Affairs Information Service
PBIP	Paper Books in Print
PBSA	Papers of the Bibliographical Society of America
PLD	Public Libraries Division
PMLA	Publications of the Modern Language Association
PNLA	Pacific Northwest Library Association
PTLA	Publishers' Trade List Annual
PW	Publishers' Weekly
RG	Readers' Guide
SEC	Securities & Exchange Commission
SLA	Special Libraries Association
SPG	Society for Propagation of the Gospel
SPGFP	Society for Propagation of the Gospel in Foreign Parts
STAR	Scientific & Technical Aerospace Reports
STC	Short-Title Catalogue
TIS	Technical Information Service
TLS	Times Literary Supplement
t.p.	title page
TVA	Tenn. Valley Authority
TWX	Teletypewriter Exchange System
UCC	Universal Copyright Convention
UDC	Universal Decimal Classification (Classification Decimale Universelle)
ULS	Union List of Serials
U.N.	United Nations
UNESCO	United Nations Educational Scientific & Cultural Organization
USAEC	United States Atomic Energy Commission
USBE	United States Book Exchange
U.S. Cat.	United States Catalog
USIA	United States Information Agency

USIS   United States Information Service

Bibliography

Coded to citation under entry; alphabetical by word or abbreviation used, with symbols listed first in their respective categories.

AA   The Americana Annual. 1923-   New York: Americana Corporation, 1923-

ALA   American Library Association. Proceedings of the Cataloging Section. Nos. 1-4. Chicago: American Library Association, 1929-1932.

ALA-B   ALA Bulletin. Vols. I-   Chicago: American Library Association, 1909-

ALA-C   American Library Association. ALA Cataloging Rules for Author and Title Entries. Edited by Clara Beetle. 7th ed. Chicago: American Library Association, 1949.

ALA-G   American Library Association. ALA Glossary of Library Terms. Compiled by Elizabeth H. Thompson. Chicago: American Library Association, 1943.

ALA-L   American Library Association. List of Subject Headings for Use in Dictionary Catalogs. Edited by Mary J. Briggs. 3d ed., revised. Chicago: American Library Association Publishing Board, 1914.

ALA-P   American Library Association. Public Library Service. Prepared by the Public Libraries Division of the Coordinating Committee on Revision of Public Library Standards. Chicago: American Library Association, 1956.

AmLA   The Bowker Annual of Library and Book

	Trade Information. 1955/56- New York: R.R. Bowker, 1956-
Adams	Adams, Randolph G. Three American-ists. Philadelphia: University of Pennsylvania Press, 1939.
Altick	Altick, Richard D. The English Common Reader; a Social History of the Mass Reading Public, 1800-1900. Chicago: University of Chicago Press, 1957.
+Altick	_____. Scholar Adventurers. New York: Macmillan, 1950.
*Altick	Altick, Richard D., and Wright, Andrew. Selective Bibliography for the Study of English and American Literature. New York: Macmillan, 1960.
Asheim	Asheim, Lester (ed.). Persistent Issues in American Librarianship. Papers presented before the Twenty-fifth Annual Conference of the Graduate Library School of the University of Chicago, August 15-17, 1960. ("University of Chicago Studies in Library Science," No. 9.) Chicago: University of Chicago Graduate Library School, 1961.
Automation	Automation and the Library of Congress. Edited for the Council on Library Resources by Gilbert W. King, et al. Washington: Library of Congress, 1963.
BB	Britannica Book of the Year. 1938- Chicago: Encyclopaedia Britannica, 1938-
Bauer	Bauer, Harry C. The Pacific Northwest Bibliographical Center. Seattle: University of Washington Press, 1950.
Bennett	Bennett, H.S. English Books and Readers, 1495-1557. Cambridge: Cambridge University Press, 1952.
Besterman	Besterman, Theodore. The Beginnings of Systematic Bibliography. London: Oxford University Press, 1935.

*Besterman   _____. A World Bibliography of Bibliographies. 2 vols. 3d ed. Metuchen, N.J.: Scarecrow Press, 1955-1956.

Beswick   Beswick, Jay W. The Work of Frederick Leypoldt, Bibliographer and Publisher. New York: R.R. Bowker, 1942.

Blades   Blades, William. Books in Chains. London: E. Stock, 1892.

Bland   Bland, David. A History of Book Illustration; the Illuminated Manuscript and the Printed Book. Cleveland: The World Publishing Co., 1958.

*Bland   _____. The Illustration of Books. 3d ed. London: Faber & Faber, 1962.

Blum   Blum, André. On the Origin of Paper. Translated by H.M. Lydenberg. New York: R.R. Bowker, 1934.

*Blum   _____. The Origins of Printing and Engraving. Translated from the French by Harry Miller Lydenberg. New York: Scribner, 1940.

Blumenthal   Blumenthal, Walter Hart. Bookmen's Bedlam. New Brunswick, N.J: Rutgers University Press, 1955.

Boaz   Boaz, Martha (ed.). Modern Trends in Documentation. Proceedings of a symposium held at the University of Southern California, April 1958. New York: Pergamon Press, 1959.

*Booth   Booth, Andrew D. Automatic Digital Calculators. New York: Academic Press, 1956.

Booth   _____. Mechanical Resolutions of Linguistic Problems. New York: Academic Press, 1958.

Bostwick   Bostwick, Arthur E. The American Public Library. New York: D. Appleton, 1910.

*Bostwick   _____. The Relationship Between the Library and the Public Schools. ("Classics of American Librarianship," vol.

	1.) White Plains, N.Y.: H.W. Wilson, 1914.
Boynton	Boynton, Henry Walcott. Annals of American Bookselling, 1638-1850. New York: John Wiley & Sons, 1932.
Branscomb	Branscomb, Harvie. Teaching With Books; a Study of College Libraries. Hamden, Conn: Shoe String Press, 1964.
Brigham	Brigham, Clarence S. Fifty Years of Collecting Americana for the Library of the American Antiquarian Society, 1908-1958. Worcester, Mass: Privately printed, 1958.
Brown	Brown, Everett S. Manual of Government Publications. New York: Appleton-Century-Crofts, 1950.
Bryan	Bryan, Alice Isabel. The Public Librarian; a Report of the Public Library Inquiry. New York: Columbia University Press, 1952.
Bryant	Bryant, Margaret M. Modern English and Its Heritage. 2d ed. New York: Macmillan, 1962.
Bühler	Bühler, Curt F.; McManaway, James G.; Wroth, Lawrence C. Standards of Bibliographical Description. Philadelphia: University of Pennsylvania Press, 1949.
Bushnell	Bushnell, George Herbert. From Papyrus to Print. London: Grafton, 1940.
*Bushnell	_____. The World's Earliest Libraries. London: Grafton, 1931.
CFP	Commission on Freedom of the Press. A Free and Responsible Press; a General Report on Mass Communication. Chicago: University of Chicago Press, 1947.
Carpenter	Carpenter, Edmund, and McLuhan, Marshall (eds.). Explorations in Communications; an Anthology. Boston: Beacon Press, 1960.

*Carter	Carter, John. ABC for Book-Collectors. New York: Knopf, 1951.
Carter	Carter, Thomas Francis. The Invention of Printing in China. Revised by L. Carrington Goodrich. New York: Ronald Press, 1955.
Casey	Casey, Robert S. (ed.). Punched Cards; Their Application to Science and Industry. 2d ed. New York: Reinhold, 1958.
Clapp	Clapp, Verner W. The Future of the Research Library. ("Phineas L. Windsor lectures in librarianship," [No. 8] 1963) Urbana, Ill: University of Illinois Press, 1964.
*Clapperton	Clapperton, R.H. Paper. Oxford: Shakespeare Head Press, 1934.
Clapperton	_____. Paper and Its Relationship to Books. London: J.M. Dent, 1934.
Clark	Clark, John Willis. The Care of Books. 2d ed. Cambridge: The University Press, 1902.
Coates	Coates, Eric James. Subject Catalogue. London: The Library Association, 1960.
Colby	Colby, Merle. A Guide to Alaska; Last American Frontier. ("Federal Writers Project: American Guide Series.") New York: Macmillan, 1939.
Collison	Collison, Robert L.W. Encyclopaedias: Their History Throughout the Ages. New York: Hafner, 1964.
*Collison	_____. Indexes and Indexing. 2d ed. London: E. Benn, 1959.
+Collison	_____. The Treatment of Special Material in Libraries. London: ASLIB, 1955.
Cooper	ALA Catalog, 1926; an Annotated Basic List of 10,000 Books. Edited by Isabella M. Cooper. Chicago: American Library Association, 1926.
Currall	Currall, Henry F.J. (ed.). Phonograph Record Libraries. Edited for the In-

194

	ternational Association of Music Libraries. Hamden, Conn: Archon Books, 1963.
Current	Current Research and Development in Scientific Documentation. No. 6. Prepared by the Office of Science Information Service. Washington: Government Printing Office, 1960.
DHL	The Dag Hammarskjold Library, Gift of the Ford Foundation. New York: United Nations, 1962.
Dance of Death	The Dance of Death: Printed at Paris in 1490. Reproduction from the copy in the Lessing J. Rosenwald collection, Library of Congress. Washington: Rare Books Division of the Library of Congress, 1945.
Daniel	Daniel, Hawthorne. Public Libraries for Everyone. Garden City, N.Y: Doubleday, 1961.
Davis	Davis, Elmer. History of the New York Times, 1851-1921. New York: New York Times, 1921.
DeVinne	DeVinne, Theodore L. The Invention of Printing. 2d ed. New York: Francis Hart, 1878.
Dewey	Dewey, Melvil. Dewey Decimal Classification and Relative Index. 2 vols. 16th ed. Lake Placid, N.Y: Forrest Press, 1959.
*Dewey	"Origins of the ALA Publishing Section," Library Notes, I, No. 2 (October, 1886), 101-104.
Doss	Doss, Milburn Price (ed.). Information Processing Equipment. New York: Reinhold, 1955.
*Downs	Downs, Robert B. (ed.). The First Freedom. Chicago: American Library Association, 1960.
+Downs	_____. Molders of the Modern Mind. New York: Barnes & Noble, 1961.
Downs	_____. Union Catalogs in the United States. Chicago: American Library

	Association, 1942.
Drake	Drake, Milton (ed.). Almanacs of the United States. 2 vols. Metuchen, N.J: Scarecrow Press, 1962.
Drury	Drury, Gertrude Gilbert. The Library and Its Organization. ("Classics of American Librarianship," [Vol. 4]) New York: H.W. Wilson, 1924.
EA	The Encyclopedia Americana. 1829- New York: Americana Corp., 1829-
EA Reprint	"Libraries," a reprint from The Encyclopedia Americana. New York: Americana Corp. [n.d.]
EB	The Encyclopaedia Britannica. 1768- Chicago: Encyclopaedia Britannica, 1768-
Eaton	Eaton, Thelma. Cataloging and Classification. 3d ed. Champaign, Ill: Illini Union Book Store, 1963.
Entiemble	Entiemble, René. The Orion Book of the Written Word. Translation of L'Ecriture, by Rebecca Abramson. New York: Orion Press, 1961.
+Esdaile	Esdaile, Arundell. The British Museum Library; a Short History and Survey. ("The Library Association series of Library Manuals IX.") London: G. Allen & Unwin, 1948.
Esdaile	_____. National Libraries of the World. 2d ed., revised. London: The Library Association, 1957.
*Esdaile	_____. A Student's Manual of Bibliography. Revised ed. London: G. Allen & Unwin, 1954.
Estienne	Estienne, Henri. The Frankfort Book Fair; the Francafordiense Emporium. Translated by James Westfall Thompson. Chicago: The Caxton Club, 1911.
Fabre	Fabre, Maurice. A History of Communication. Translated by Peter Chaitin. ("The New Illustrated Library of Science and Invention," No.

	9.) New York: Hawthorne Books, 1963.
Feipel	Feipel, Louis Nicholas, and Browning, Earl W. Library Binding Manual. Chicago: American Library Association, 1951.
Free Lib. Phil.	One Hundred and Fifty Years of Printing in English America, (1640-1790). Philadelphia: Free Library of Philadelphia, 1940.
French	French, John Calvin. The Johns Hopkins Press. Baltimore: Johns Hopkins Press, 1938.
Fussler	Fussler, Herman H. (ed.). Library Buildings for Library Service. Papers presented before the Library Institute at the University of Chicago, Aug. 5-10, 1946. Chicago: American Library Association, 1947.
Garceau	Garceau, Oliver; Hardy, C. Dewitt; et al. The Public Library in the Political Process; a Report of the Public Library Inquiry. New York: Columbia University Press, 1949.
Garnett	Garnett, Richard. Essays in Librarianship and Bibliography. ("The Library Series," No. 5.) London: G. Allen, 1899.
Geer	Geer, Helen Thornton. Charging Systems. Chicago: American Library Association, 1955.
Glaister	Glaister, Geoffrey A. Glossary of the Book. London: G. Allen & Unwin, 1960.
Grattan	Grattan, C. Hartley (ed.). American Ideas About Adult Education, 1710-1951. ("Classics in Education," No. 2.) New York: Teacher's College, Columbia University, 1959.
Greenberger	Greenberger, Martin (ed.). Computers and the World of the Future. Cambridge, Mass: MIT Press, 1962.
*Growoll	Growoll, Adolf. American Book Clubs;

	Their Beginnings and History and a Bibliography of Their Publications. ("Burt Franklin Bibliography and Reference series," No. 77.) New York: Burt Franklin [n.d.] [originally published Dodd, Mead, 1897]
Growoll	_____. Book Trade Bibliography in the United States in the Nineteenth Century. Reprinted 1939 in an edition of 150 copies. New York: The Brick Row Book Shop.
Haebler	Haebler, Konrad. The Story of Incunabula. Translated by Lucy Eugenia Osborne. New York: The Grolier Club, 1933.
Hamer	U.S. National Historical Publications Commission. A Guide to Archives and Manuscripts. Edited for the Commission by Philip M. Hamer. New Haven, Conn: Yale University Press, 1961.
Harrod	Harrod, Leonard M. The Librarians' Glossary. London: Grafton, 1959.
Hawley	Hawley, George F. Automating the Manufacturing Process. New York: Reinhold, 1959.
Herdeg	Herdeg, Walter. Art in the Watermark. Zurich: Amstutz and Herdeg, 1952.
Hessel	Hessel, Alfred. A History of Libraries. Translated by Reuben Peiss. Metuchen, N.J: Scarecrow Press, 1950.
Hirsch	Hirsch, S. Carl. This Is Automation. New York: Viking Press, 1964.
Hocking	Hocking, William Ernst. Freedom of the Press; a Framework of Principle. Report from the Commission on Freedom of the Press. Chicago: University of Chicago Press, 1948.
Hofer	Hofer, Philip. Eighteenth Century Book Illustrations. ("The Augustan Reprints," No. 58.) Los Angeles: Wm. Anders Clark Memorial Library, University of California, 1956.

Hoffman	Hoffman, Hester R. (ed.). The Reader's Adviser and Bookman's Manual. 9th ed. New York: R.R. Bowker, 1960.
Holden	Holden, John A. The Bookman's Glossary. 2d ed. New York: R.R. Bowker, 1931.
Hower	Hower, Ralph M. The History of an Advertising Agency. Revised ed. Cambridge, Mass: Harvard University Press, 1949.
+Hunter	Hunter, Dard. Papermaking. New York: Knopf, 1943.
Hunter	_____. Papermaking in Pioneer America. Philadelphia: University of Pennsylvania Press, 1952.
*Hunter	_____. Papermaking Through Eighteen Centuries. New York: Wm. Edwin Rudge, 1930.
Huxley	Huxley, Julian. UNESCO: Its Purposes and Its Philosophy. Washington: Public Affairs Press, 1947.
*Irwin	Irwin, Raymond. The Heritage of the English Library. New York: Hafner, 1964.
+Irwin	_____. The National Library Service. London: Grafton, 1947.
Irwin	_____. The Origins of the English Library. London: G. Allen & Unwin, 1958.
#Irwin	Irwin, Raymond, and Staveley, Ronald (eds.). The Libraries of London. 2d ed. revised. London: The Library Association, 1961.
Joeckel	Joeckel, Carleton B. The Government of the American Public Library. Chicago: University of Chicago Press, 1935.
Johnson	Johnson, Elmer D. A History of Libraries in the Western World. Metuchen, N.J: Scarecrow Press, 1965.
Kainen	Kainen, Jacob. John Baptist Jackson. Washington: Government Printing Of-

fice, 1962.

Kenyon Kenyon, Frederick G. Books and Their Readers in Ancient Greece and Rome. 2d ed. Oxford: Clarendon Press, 1951.

Kerr Kerr, Chester. A Report on American University Presses. [Chicago:] Association of American University Presses, 1949.

Kimber Kimber, Sidney A. The Story of an Old Press. Cambridge, Mass: The University Press [1937].

Kingery Kingery, Robert E., and Tauber, Maurice F. (eds.). Book Catalogs. Metuchen, N.J: Scarecrow Press, 1962.

Kull Kull, Irving S. A Short Chronology of American History, 1492-1950. New Brunswick, N.J: Rutgers University Press, 1952.

LAA Libraries and Automation. Proceedings of the Conference on Libraries and Automation held at Airlie Foundation, Warrenton, Va., May 26-30, 1963. Edited by Barbara Evans Markerson. Washington: The Library of Congress, 1964.

LADP Library Application of Data Processing Clinic, University of Illinois Graduate School of Library Science, April 28-May 1, 1963. Proceedings. Edited by Herbert Goldhor. Champaign, Ill: The Illini Union Bookstore, 1964.

LCIB Information Bulletin. Vols. I- Washington: The Library of Congress, 1942-

Labarre Labarre, E.J. A Dictionary of Paper and Papermaking Terms. Amsterdam: N.V. Swets & Zeitlinger, 1937.

Lamb Lamb, C.M., et al. (eds.). The Calligraphers Handbook. London: Faber & Faber, 1956.

Langer Langer, Wm. Leonard (ed.). An Encyclopedia of World History. Boston:

Houghton Mifflin, 1952.

Laves   Laves, Walter H.C., and Thomson, Charles A. <u>Unesco</u>. Bloomington, Ind: Indiana University Press, 1957.

Lawler   Lawler, John. <u>The H.W. Wilson Company; Half a Century of Bibliographic Publishing</u>. Minneapolis: University of Minn. Press, 1950.

Lehmann   Lehmann-Haupt, Hellmut. <u>The Book in America; à History of the Making and Selling of Books in the United States.</u> 2d ed. New York: R.R. Bowker, 1951.

Leidy   Leidy, William Philip. <u>A Popular Guide to Government Publications.</u> New York: Columbia University Press, 1953.

Leigh   Leigh, Robert Devore. <u>The Public Library in the United States; the General Report of the Public Library Inquiry.</u> New York: Columbia University Press, 1950.

*Leigh   _____ (ed.). <u>Major Problems in the Education of Librarians.</u> New York: Columbia University Press, 1954.

Libri   <u>Libri</u>. Vols. I- Copenhagen: 1950-

LibJ   <u>Library Journal</u>. Vols. I- New York: R.R. Bowker, 1876-

LibQ   <u>The Library Quarterly</u>. Vols. I- Chicago: University of Chicago Press, 1931

Library   <u>The Library; a Quarterly Review of Bibliography.</u> Ser. I- vols. 1- London: Oxford University Press, 1889-

LibT   <u>Library Trends</u>. Vols. I- Urbana, Ill: University of Illinois Press, 1952-

Licklider   Licklider, J.C.R. <u>Libraries of the Future.</u> Cambridge, Mass: MIT Press, 1965.

Linder   Linder, LeRoy Harold. <u>The Rise of Current Complete National Bibliography.</u>

	Metuchen, N.J: Scarecrow Press, 1959.
Lucas	Lucas, Mary Rinehart. The Organization and Administration of Library Service to Children. M.A. dissertation, published. Chicago: American Library Association, 1941.
McGraw	McGraw-Hill Encyclopedia of Science and Technology. 15 vols. New York: McGraw-Hill, 1960.
Machlup	Machlup, Fritz. The Production and Distribution of Knowledge in the United States. Princeton, N.J: Princeton University Press, 1962.
McKerrow	McKerrow, Ronald. Introduction to Bibliography for Literary Students. Oxford: Clarendon Press, 1927.
McMurtrie	McMurtrie, Douglas C. The Book. 3d ed. New York: Oxford University Press, 1943.
Malclès	Malclès, Louise N. Bibliographic Service Throughout the World. 1st and 2d annual reports. Paris: UNESCO, 1955.
Mann	Mann, George. Print; a Manual for Librarians and Students. London: Grafton, 1952.
*Mann	Mann, Margaret. Introduction to Cataloging and the Classification of Books. 2d ed. Chicago: American Library Association, 1943.
Marshall	Marshall, John David (ed.). An American Library History Reader. ("Contributions to Library Literature," No. 5.) Hamden, Conn: Shoe String Press, 1961.
Mason	Mason, Donald. A Primer of Non-book Material in Libraries. London: Association of Assistant Librarians, 1959.
Mayer	Mayer, Alfred. Annals of European Civilization 1501-1900. London: Cassell, 1949.

Mearns   Mearns, David C. The Story Up to
Now; The Library of Congress 1800-
1946. Washington: The Library of
Congress, 1947.

Meltzer   Meltzer, Milton (ed.). Milestones to
American Liberty. New York:
Crowell, 1961.

Metcalfe   Metcalfe, John Wallace. Subject Cataloging and Indexing of Libraries and
Literature. Metuchen, N.J: Scarecrow Press, 1959.

Miller   Miller, William. The Book Industry; a
Report of the Public Library Inquiry.
New York: Columbia University
Press, 1949.

Minn.   Minnesota University Press. Ten Years
of Publishing. Minneapolis: University of Minn. Press, 1937.

Morison   Morison, Samuel Eliot. The Founding
of Harvard College. Cambridge,
Mass: Harvard University Press,
1935.

Mulgan   Mulgan, John, and Davin, D.M. An Introduction to English Literature. Oxford: Clarendon Press, 1961.

Nicholson   Nicholson, Margaret. A Manual of Copyright Practice for Writers, Publishers,
and Agents. London: Oxford University Press, 1945.

19th cent.   Nineteenth-Century English Books; Some
Problems in Bibliography. ("Windsor
lectures in librarianship," No. 3.)
Urbana, Ill: University of Illinois
Press, 1952.

Oswald   Oswald, John Clyde. Printing in the
Americas. New York: Gregg Pub-
lishing Co., 1937.

PW   The Publishers' Weekly. Vols. I-
New York: R.R. Bowker, 1872-

*PW   _____. 500 Years of Printing. New
York: Printing Advisory Committee
of the American Institute of Graphic
Arts, 1940.

Parsons   Parsons, Edward Alexander. The Alex-
               andrian Library. New York: The
               Elsevier Press, 1952.
Peddie   Peddie, R.A. (ed.). Printing, a Short
               History of the Art. London: Grafton,
               1927.
Pettee   Pettee, Julia. Subject Headings. New
               York: H.W. Wilson, 1947.
Pinner   Pinner, H. L. The World of Books in
               Classical Antiquity. Leiden: A.W.
               Sijthoff, 1948.
Pollard   Pollard, Alfred W. Early Illustrated
               Books. 3d ed. London: Kegan Paul,
               Trench, Trubner, 1926.
Powell   Powell, John H. The Books of a New
               Nation. Philadelphia: University of
               Pennsylvania Press, 1957.
Predeek   Predeek, Albert. A History of Librar-
               ies in Great Britain and North Amer-
               ica. Translated by Lawrence S.
               Thompson. Chicago: American Li-
               brary Association, 1947.
*Putnam   Putnam, George Haven. Authors and
               Their Public in Ancient Times. 3d
               ed., revised. New York: G. P. Put-
               nam's Sons, 1923.
+Putnam   _____. Books and Their Makers
               During the Middle Ages. 2 vols. 2d
               ed. New York: G. P. Putnam's Sons,
               1896.
Putnam   _____. The Question of Copyright.
               New York: G. P. Putnam's Sons,
               1891.
QuarJ   The Quarterly Journal of the Library of
               Congress. Supplement to the Annual
               Report of the Librarian of Congress.
               Vols. I-   Washington: The Library
               of Congress, 1943-
Randall   Randall, Wm. M. The College Library.
               Chicago: American Library Associa-
               tion, 1932.
Ranz   Ranz, Jim. The Printed Book Catalogue
               in American Libraries: 1723-1900.

("ACRL Monograph, " No. 26.) Chicago: American Library Association, 1964.

Richardson   Richardson, Ernest Cushing. <u>The Beginnings of Libraries.</u> Hamden, Conn: Archon Books, 1963.

*Richardson   . <u>Biblical Libraries: a Sketch of Library History From 3400 B. C. to A. D. 150.</u> Hamden, Conn: Archon Books, 1963.

Rider   Rider, Fremont. <u>The Scholar and the Future of the Research Library.</u> New York: Hedham Press, 1944.

Rogers   Rogers, Joseph W. <u>U.S. National Bibliography and the Copyright Law.</u> New York: R.R. Bowker, 1960.

Rosner   Rosner, Charles. <u>The Growth of the Book Jacket.</u> Cambridge, Mass: Harvard Press, 1954.

SE-Lib   <u>The Southeastern Librarian.</u> Vols I- Atlanta: Southeastern Library Association, 1951-

Savage   Savage, Ernst A. <u>Old English Libraries.</u> ("The Antiquary's Books.") London: Mitchum, 1911.

Saville   Saville, Max. <u>A Short History of American Civilization.</u> New York: Holt, Rinehart and Winston, 1957.

Sayers   Sayers, William Charles Berwick. <u>A Manual of Classification for Librarians and Bibliographers.</u> 3d ed., revised. London: Grafton, 1955.

Schellenberg   Schellenberg, Theodore R. <u>The Management of Archives.</u> ("Columbia University Studies in Library Service, " No. 14.) New York: Columbia University Press, 1965.

*Schellenberg   . <u>Modern Archives; Principles and Techniques.</u> Chicago: University of Chicago Press, 1956.

Schmeckebier   Schmeckebier, Laurence F. , and Eastin, Roy B. <u>Government Publications and Their Use.</u> Revised ed. Washington:

	Brookings Institution, 1961.
Schultheiss	Schultheiss, Louis A.; Culbertson, Don S.; Heiliger, Edward M. Advanced Data Processing in the University Library. Metuchen, N.J: Scarecrow Press, 1962.
Sears	Sears, Helen L. American University Presses Come of Age. Syracuse, N.Y: Syracuse University Press, 1959.
Sharp	Sharp, Harold S. (ed.). Readings in Information Retrieval. Metuchen, N.J: Scarecrow Press, 1964.
Shaw	Shaw, Ralph Robert, and Shoemaker, Richard H. American Bibliography, 1801-1819. 19 vols. Metuchen, N.J: Scarecrow Press, 1958-1963.
+Shaw	_____. Literary Property in the United States. Metuchen, N.J: Scarecrow Press, 1950.
*Shaw	_____. The Use of Photography for Clerical Routines. A report to the American Council of Learned Societies. Washington: American Council of Learned Societies, 1953.
Shera	Shera, Jesse H. Foundations of the Public Library; the Origins of the Public Library Movement in New England, 1629-1855. Chicago: University of Chicago Press, 1949.
Shores	Shores, Louis. Origins of the American College Library, 1638-1800. ("Contribution to education," No. 134.) Hamden, Conn: Shoe String Press, 1966.
Shove	Shove, Raymond H., et al. The Use of Books and Libraries. 10th ed. Minneapolis: University of Minn. Press, 1963.
Sledd	Sledd, James, and Ebbitt, Wilma R. Dictionaries and That Dictionary. Chicago: Scott, Foresman, 1962.
Smith	Smith, Roger H. (ed.). The American Reading Public; Daedalus Symposium. New York: R.R. Bowker, 1964.

Sonnenschein	Sonnenschein, Wm. Swan. <u>The Best</u> <u>Books</u>. 3 vols. 3d ed. London: G. Routledge, 1910.
Spielmann	Spielmann, Percy Edwin (comp.). <u>Cat-</u> <u>alogue of the Library of Miniature</u> <u>Books</u>. London: Edward Arnold, 1961.
Steinberg	Steinberg, S. H. <u>Five Hundred Years</u> <u>of Printing</u>. New York: Criterion Books, 1959.
*Steinberg	_____. <u>Historical Tables 58BC-AD</u> <u>1958</u>. London: Macmillan, 1959.
Stillwell	Stillwell, Margaret Bingham. <u>Incuna-</u> <u>bula and Americana, 1450-1800; a Key</u> <u>to Bibliographical Study</u>. New York: Columbia University Press, 1931.
Strout	Strout, Ruth French (ed.). <u>Toward a</u> <u>Better Cataloging Code</u>. Chicago: University of Chicago Graduate Li- brary School, 1957.
Sutermeister	Sutermeister, Edwin. <u>Story of Paper-</u> <u>making</u>. Boston: S.D. Warren, 1954.
Talboys	Talboys, David A. <u>Annales Antiquitatis;</u> <u>Chronological Tables of Ancient His-</u> <u>tory</u>. Oxford: D.A. Talboys, 1838.
Tauber	Tauber, Maurice F. <u>Technical Services</u> <u>in Libraries</u>. New York: Columbia University Press, 1953.
Taylor	Taylor, Archer. <u>Book Catalogues;</u> <u>Their Varieties and Use</u>. Chicago: The Newberry Library, 1957.
Thomas	Thomas, Isaiah. <u>The History of Print-</u> <u>ing in America</u>. 2 vols. 2d ed. (American Antiquarian Society. Trans- actions and Collections. Vol. 5.) Albany, N.Y: Joel Munsell, 1874- 187?
⊘Thompson	Thompson, C. Seymour. <u>Evolution of</u> <u>the American Public Library 1653-</u> <u>1876</u>. Metuchen, N.J: Scarecrow Press, 1952.
*Thompson	Thompson, James Westfall. <u>Ancient Li-</u> <u>braries</u>. Berkeley: University of

	California Press, 1940.
Thompson	_____. The Medieval Library. ("The University of Chicago Studies in Library Science.") Chicago: University of Chicago Press, 1939.
#Thompson	Thompson, Lawrence S. Printing in Colonial Spanish America. Hamden, Conn: Shoe String Press, 1962.
+Thompson	Thompson, Oscar (ed.). The International Cyclopedia of Music and Musicians. Revised ed. New York: Dodd, Mead, 1958.
Thornton	Thornton, John L. The Chronology of Librarianship. London: Grafton, 1941.
+Thornton	_____. Classics of Librarianship. London: The Library Association, 1957.
*Thornton	_____. A Mirror for Librarians. London: Grafton, 1948.
Timperley	Timperley, C.H. A Dictionary of Printers and Printing. London: H. Johnson, 1839.
*Timperley	_____. Encyclopaedia of Literary and Typographical Anecdote. 2d ed. London: H.G. Bohn, 1842.
Tsien	Tsien, Tsuen-Hsuin. Written on Bamboo and Silk. ("The University of Chicago Studies in Library Science.") Chicago: University of Chicago Press, 1962.
UBL	Unesco Bulletin for Libraries. Vols. I- Paris: UNESCO, 1948-
ULM	Union List of Microfilms. Prepared by the Philadelphia Bibliographical Center and Union Library Catalogue. Revised. Ann Arbor, Mich: J.W. Edwards, 1951.
Unesco	Reflections on Our Age: Lectures Delivered at the Opening Session of Unesco at the Sorbonne University, Paris. New York: Columbia University Press, 1949.
USLC	The Cataloging-in-Source Experiment.

	A report to the Librarian of Congress by the Director of the Processing Department. Washington: The Library of Congress, 1960.
Ullman	Ullman, B. L. Ancient Writing and Its Influence. ("Our Debt to Greece and Rome.") New York: Longmans, Green, 1932.
Ulrich	Ulrich's Periodical Directory. 10th ed. Edited by Eileen C. Graves. New York: R.R. Bowker, 1963.
Updike	Updike, Daniel Berkeley. Printing Types, Their History, Form, and Use. 2 vols. Cambridge, Mass: Harvard University Press, 1962.
Utley	Utley, George B. Fifty Years of the American Library Association. Chicago: American Library Association, 1926.
Walls	Walls, Howard. The Copyright Handbook for Fine and Applied Arts. New York: Watson-Guptill, 1963.
Weeks	Weeks, Lyman H. History of Papermaking in the U.S.A. 1690-1916. New York: Lakewood Trade Journal, 1916.
Weitzmann	Weitzmann, Kurt. Ancient Book Illumination. ("Martin Classical Lectures," Vol. XVI.) Cambridge, Mass: Harvard University Press, 1959.
White	White, Carl Milton. The Origins of the American Library School. Metuchen, N.J: Scarecrow Press, 1961.
Williams	Williams, Edwin E. Farmington Plan Handbook. Bloomington, Ind: Association of Research Libraries, 1933.
Williamson	Williamson, William L. William Frederick Poole and the Modern Library Movement. New York: Columbia University Press, 1963.
Wilson	Wilson, Louis Round. The Geography of Reading. Chicago: American Library Association, 1938.
Winchell	Winchell, Constance M. Guide to Ref-

erence Books. 7th ed. Chicago:
American Library Association, 1951.

Wincor   Wincor, Richard. From Ritual to Roy-
             alties. New York: Walker & Co.,
             1962.

Winship   Winship, George Parker. Gutenberg to
             Plantin. Cambridge, Mass: Harvard
             University Press, 1926.

Wormald   Wormald, Francis, and Wright, C.E.
             (eds.). The English Library Before
             1700. London: University of London,
             1958.

Wroth   Wroth, Lawrence C. The Colonial
             Printer. Portland, Maine: South-
             worth-Anthoensen Press, 1938.

Wyer   Wyer, James I. Reference Work. Chi-
             cago: American Library Association,
             1930.

Subject Index

The Subject Index proposes to pull together the varied facts presented in the Tables, under broad headings suggesting the many aspects of librarianship, including science, service and economy, i.e., husbandry. It should never be used in place of the Tables; the date is given in lieu of a page number, and means "a source" not "the information." The Name Index should be used for a distinctive name or title.

Aid (funds) cont.
  Municipal 1810; 1827; 1848; 1849
  State 1827; 1833; 1835
  Tax (excise) 1734
Almanac see Reference tools
Alphabet see Transcribing medium
Alphabetic arrangement 1700
American libraries abroad 1920; 1942; 1944; 1945; 1948
Analytics (cat.) see Cataloging
Annuals see Reference tools
Apprentice classes see Education
Apprentices' library see Mechanics' Library Move-
   ment
Appropriations see Aid (funds)
Architecture 1627; 1661; 1706; 1750; 1785; 1835; 1840;
   1843; 1852; 1854; 1914; 1931; 1932; 1933; 1944
  see also Carrels, Shelving
Archives 1790; 1895; 1899; 1906; 1934; 1938; 1948
Associations 1853
   AALS 1915
   AASL 1915
   ACRL 1889
   ALA 1876
   ARL 1931
   ASLIB 1924
   Agri. librarians 1955
   Archives 1906; 1948
   Bibl. Soc. of Am. 1904
   CNLA 1942
   Catholic 1921
   Educ. Film 1943
   FID 1892
   Hospital 1944
   IFLA 1929
   Inter-Am. 1930
   Int. Lib. Com. 1927
   Jewish 1946
   Law 1906
   Library Assoc. (Eng.) 1877
   Medical 1898
   Merchant Marine. 1921
   Mt. Plains. 1948
   Music 1931; 1951

Associations cont.

Book: Form & Make-up cont.
    Running titles 1490
    Signatures 1472
    Table of contents 1470
    Title-page 800; 1463; 1470; 1476
    see also Decoration (bk.); Illustration (bk.)
Book club 1800; 1926
Book collectors (private) 1484
Book selection 1793; 1887; 1905; 1908; 1909; 1921;
    1924; 1930
    Cooperative 1893
    Reference tools 1902; 1910; 1930; 1941
Book trade 1st cent.; 1462; 1470; 1472; 1539; 1557;
    1647; 1657; 1919; 1954; 1955; 1958
    Advertisement 1466; 1469; 1477; 1479; 1498;
    1564; 1804
    Antiquarian 1906; 1948; 1949
    Association 1st cent.; 1724; 1801; 1900; 1906;
    1946; 1949
    Best seller 1473
    Blurb 1476; 1906
    Company (pub.) 1472; 1785
    Device (pr.) 1462; 1539
    Dust jacket 1833; 1906
    Fairs 1473; 1564; 1802; 1919; 1949
Bookmark 1400
Bookmobile see Extension service
Bookplate see Ex libris
Braille writing see Service-to-the-handicapped
Branch library see Extension service
Bray library see Colonial library
Broadcasting see Public relations: Radio
Browsing room 1930
Business library see Special Library Movement
Call number see Cataloging
Card copy program (LC) 1902; 1910
Card distribution 1893; 1901; 1938
    ALA card 1887; 1893
    LC card 1901; 1902; 1910; 1930; 1959
Carnegie aid 1881; 1889; 1911
Carrels 1370; 1915
Cataloging 831; 1250; 1389; 1400; 1412; 1494; 1558;
    1560; 1853; 1875; 1891; 1901; 1926; 1930; 1957

Classification systems cont.

Education cont.
>ALA Committee 1889
>Accreditation 1924; 1948; 1951; 1952; 1958
>Apprentice classes 1891; 1905; 1914
>Certification see main entry
>Children's librarian 1901
>Curriculum 1884; 1898; 1901; 1903; 1905; 1915; 1939
>>Extra-curricula 1883; 1947; 1958
>Dana report 1900
>Degrees 1889; 1928
>Fifth-year program 1905
>Formal study 1865; 1874; 1884; 1891; 1895
>Fraternities see main entry
>Graduate program 1902; 1928
>In-service 1896
>Princeton Conference 1948
>Recruiting programs see main entry
>School librarian 1915
>Schools (representative listing) 1887; 1924; 1925; 1951
>>Accredited
>>>Atlanta University 1941
>>>California 1919
>>>Calif. (UCLA) 1953
>>>Carnegie Tech. 1901
>>>Catholic University 1938
>>>Chicago 1927
>>>Columbia 1887
>>>Denver 1931
>>>Drexel 1891
>>>Emory 1905
>>>Florida State 1947
>>>George Peabody 1928
>>>Illinois 1893
>>>Indiana 1949
>>>Kentucky 1933
>>>Louisiana State 1931
>>>Michigan 1926
>>>Minnesota 1928
>>>North Carolina 1931
>>>Oklahoma 1929
>>>Pratt Institute 1890

Education cont.
  Accredited schools
    Rosary College 1953
    Rutgers 1953
    Simmons 1902
    Southern Calif. 1936
    State U. of N.Y. 1953
    Syracuse 1908
    Texas Woman's Univ. 1929
    Univ. of Pittsburg 1953
    Univ. of Texas 1948
    Washington 1911
    Western Michigan 1953
    Western Reserve 1953
    Wisconsin. 1904
  Standards 1925; 1951; 1952; 1958
  3-plus-1 program 1920
  Williamson report 1923
Effects of reading, Physical 1945; 1957
Encyclopedia see Reference tools
End sheets see Book: Form & Make-up
Engraving see Illustration (bk.)
Errata see Book: Form & Make-up
Ethics 1938
Ex libris 1450
Exceptional children see Public Library Movement
Exchange programs (materials) 1694; 1811; 1832; 1840;
  1867; 1946
  Duplicates 1694; 1840; 1948
Extension services 1869; 1890; 1956
  Bookmobile 1905
  Branch 1871
  Commission 1890
  Package 1905
  see also County library service; Traveling li-
   brary
Facsimile processes
  Photography 1839
  Press printing
   Seals 450
   Blocks 700
   Types 1041
  Rubbings 175

Facsimile processes cont.
    Television 1951
Fairs   see   Book trade
Federal aid   see   Aid (funds)
Federal library   1777; 1789; 1803; 1832; 1836; 1850;
      1853; 1862; 1870; 1882; 1895
    Agriculture   1860; 1889; 1942
    Armed Forces   1952
    Army Medical   1922
    Library of Congress   1789; 1800; 1802; 1814; 1815;
      1824; 1830; 1832; 1851; 1865; 1866; 1867; 1897;
      1898; 1901; 1907; 1915; 1921; 1924; 1939; 1942;
      1943; 1945; 1952; 1954; 1955; 1957
      see also   Catalogs: LC; Card distribution
    Military   1777; 1845; 1861
    National Archives   1934
    National Library of Medicine   1956
    OWI libraries   1942; 1944; 1945
      see also below USIS
    Presidents' libraries   1955
    Smithsonian   1846; 1866; 1875
    Surgeon General's Office   1836; 1879; 1880
    USIA   see below USIS
    USIS   1948
    White House   1809
Federal relations   1938; 1945; 1958
    Aid   see   main entry
    Customs   1953
    Postal rates   1904; 1938; 1958
Fifth-year program   see   Education
Filing equipment   1868
Film (material)   see Photo-reproduction; Special Li-
      brary service
Film library service   see   Special Library service
Finding lists   see   Catalogs: Printed: Variants
Fines   see   Administration: Regulations
Foliation   see   Book: Form & Make-up
Fraternities   1903; 1948; 1950; 1954
Freedom of the press   see   Censorship
Freedom to read   see   Censorship
Friends-of-the-library   see   Public relations
Glossary   see   Reference service

Lending library   see   Circulating library
Librarian   1412; 1650; 1667; 1681; 1732; 1802; 1815;
        1838; 1853; 1856; 1861; 1897; 1905; 1910; 1930
    Certification   see   main entry
    Education   see   main entry
    see also   Administration; Association: Staff
Libraries abroad   see   American libraries abroad
Library bulletins   see   Catalogs: Printed: Variants
Library economy   see   Administration
Library schools   see   Education
Linotype   see   Printing: Mechanical
Literacy and learning   597; 668; 1400; 1514
Lithographs   see   Illustration (bk.)
Lithography   see   Printing
Loans (bk.)   see   Administration
Lobby   see   Federal relations
Lyceum movement   see   Adult education
Magazine   see   Serial publication: Periodical
Mail order library   see   Extention service: Package
Management (lib.)   see   Administration
Manual   1539
Mechanics' Library Movement   1818; 1820; 1829; 1833;
        1855
Mechanization   1877
    Binding   1908
    Charging systems   see   main entry
    Inter-library lending   1950
    Library management   1876
        Technical processes   1953
    Paper   see   main entry
    Phono-reproduction   see   main entry
    Printing   see   main entry
    Retrieval systems   see   Automation
    Shelving   1887
    Transcribing tools   see   main entry
    Translation service   see   Automation
Medical library   see   Special Library service
Mercantile Library Movement   1818; 1820; 1821; 1839;
        1843; 1846; 1853; 1857
Micro-reproduction   see   Photo-reproduction
Miniature book   see   Book: Form & Make-up
Monastic library   see   Christian religion: Influence
Motion picture   see   Non-book materials

Non-book material cont.
    Forms
        Motion picture 1894; 1954; 1958
        Music see Phono-reproduction; Printing: Music symbols; Special Library service
        Newspaper see Serial publication
        Pamphlet 1712; 1958
           Checklist 1910; 1932
        Periodicals see Serial publication
        Phono-forms see Phono-reproduction
        Photo-forms see Photo-reproduction
        Pictures see Special Library service; Illustration (bk.)
        Prints see Special Library service: Pictures
        Punched cards see Automation
        Talking-book 1934
           see also Phono-reproduction
        Vocals (live) see Radio; Television; Story-telling
Numeral system 1100
Open shelves practice 1879
Overseas libraries see American libraries abroad
Package library see Extension services
Pagination see Book: Form & Make-up
Pamphlet see Non-book material
Paper 1st cent; 105; 1109; 1221; 1309; 1866
    Binding 1500; 1579
    Carbon 1905
    Machine 1798; 1805; 1809; 1816; 1825; 1827
    Mills 753; 1150; 1276; 1492; 1690
    Varieties 1465; 1625; 1750; 1757; 1768; 1800; 1869; 1874
        see also below Wood
    Watermarks 1282
    Wood 1719; 1830
Patients' library see Service-to-the-handicapped: Hospital
Pens (writing) see Transcribing tool
Periodical see Serial publication
Personnel see Librarian
Philanthropies (public lib.)
    Bequests see Public Library Movement
    Bray 1698

Presses   see   Printing; University press service
Printing   175; 450; 932; 935; 1455; 1473; 1476; 1484;
       1499; 1539; 1620; 1775; 1813; 1908
   Block printing   700; 868; 1423
   see also   Illustration (bk.)
   Color   1457; 1482; 1486; 1711; 1718
   Gothic type   1510
   Greek letters   1465; 1543
   Ink   1st cent.; 400; 1100; 1813
   Italic type   1500; 1501
   Lithography   1796; 1813; 1818; 1828
   Math symbols   1482
   Miniature type   1850
   Measure unit   1737
   Mechanical   1790; 1803; 1812; 1821; 1846; 1865;
       1884
   Movable type   1041; 1298; 1370; 1392; 1440; 1444;
       1448; 1454; 1850
   Music symbols   1476; 1750
   Offset   1875; 1904
   Photo-composing   1928; 1948; 1951; 1959
   Proofs   1458
   Reduced printing   1460; 1500; 1934
       Pocket editions   1501
   Reflex   1839
   Reforms   1674; 1787
   Reprints (mass production)   175; 450; 600; 868;
       932; 1454; 1844
   Roman type   1467; 1518; 1769
   Specimen sheet (type)   1469
   Type foundry   1392; 1579; 1769
   Type plates   1725; 1781; 1800; 1812; 1813; 1816;
       1850
   U.S.   1638; 1639; 1640; 1775
   University press service   see   main entry
   Xerography   1938
Prints library   see   Special Library service: Picture
Prison libraries   1930; 1938; 1944; 1950
Professional journals (representative listing)   1876;
       1889; 1907; 1908; 1910; 1911; 1914; 1931; 1934;
       1938; 1939; 1942; 1943; 1949; 1950; 1952; 1953;
       1957; 1959
Propaganda agent   1847; 1871; 1920; 1924; 1942; 1944;

Propaganda agent cont.
        1945; 1948; 1949; 1951; 1954; 1955; 1956; 1957
Proprietary library   see   Social Library Movement
Public Library Movement   1st cent.; 1473; 1524; 1601;
        1698; 1854; 1859; 1871; 1881
    Administration   see   main entry
    Aid   see   main entry
    Bequests   1436; 1657; 1713; 1730; 1747; 1803
    Children's service   1804; 1807; 1885; 1894; 1899;
        1900; 1901
    Costs   1959
    Defined   1850; 1871; 1928
    Exceptional children   1959
    Legislation   see   main entry
    Reading improvement   1953
    School district   1835
    Standards   1921; 1933; 1943; 1948; 1956; 1959
    Storytelling   1899
    Surveys   1876; 1926; 1949
    Trustees   1852; 1878; 1890
    Young adult service   1919; 1920
    U.S. (representative listing)
        Alaska 1900
        Boston 1854
        Buffalo 1897
        Chicago 1872
        Cincinnati 1856
        Cleveland 1869
        Detroit 1865
        Enoch Pratt, Baltimore 1882
        Hawaii 1913
        Indianapolis 1868
        Los Angeles 1872
        Milwaukee 1875
        Minneapolis 1885
        New York 1895
        Newark, N.J. 1889
        Phila. Free Lib. 1891
        Pittsburgh (Carnegie) 1881
        Pratt Inst. Free Lib. 1887
        Providence, R.I. 1878
        St. Louis 1865
        San Juan, Puerto Rico 1899

Regional catalogs see Union catalog service
Regional lists of serials see Union list service
Regulations (lib.) see Administration
Religion: Influence see Christian religion: Influence
Rental library see Circulating library
Reprints (mass production) see Printing
Research 1956; 1959
Research libraries (representative listing) 1846; 1887;
     1897; 1904; 1919; 1924; 1932
    Endowed reference libraries 1857; 1858; 1859;
     1889; 1907; 1912; 1923; 1946
Reserve book program see Administration
Retrieval systems
    Automation see main entry
    Classification see main entry
    Index see Index services
    Loan see Inter-library lending
    Photo-duplication see Photo-reproduction
    see also Bibliography; Catalogs
Revolving library see Traveling library
Rubbings see Printing
Rules (lib.) see Administration: Regulations
Running titles see Book: Form & Make-up
Rural reading 1951
Scholarly society libraries see Colonial libraries
School library 1827; 1915; 1952
    Elementary 1925
    Secondary 1905; 1920; 1927
    Standards 1920; 1925; 1927
Script see Transcribing medium
Seals see Facsimile processes
Selective retirement see Weeding
Seminary library see Special Library service: Theo-
    logical
Serial publication
    Checklists 1876; 1880; 1892; 1899; 1927; 1930;
     1932; 1947; 1951; 1957
    Indices 1848; 1853; 1882; 1883; 1896; 1901; 1913
    Installment basis 1678
    Micro-film 1933; 1938; 1955; 1957
    Newspaper 400; 1513; 1621; 1689; 1933; 1947;
     1955; 1957
    Periodical 1663; 1665; 1691; 1724; 1918; 1930

Service-to-the-blind   see   Service-to-the-handicapped
Service-to-the-handicapped   1959
        Bibliotherapy   1941
        Blind   1868; 1904; 1931; 1954
            Braille writing   1829; 1952
            Talking-book   1934
        Deaf   1958
        Hospital   1811; 1944
        Shut-ins   1941
Shelving   1584
        Compact   1887; 1958
        Stacks   1854
        Tiers   1785
Shut-ins   see   Service-to-the-handicapped
Signatures (marks)   see   Book: Form & Make-up
Social Library Movement   1710; 1731; 1849
        Corporation   1742; 1747; 1796; 1798
        Ladies' library   1850
        Student societies   1769; 1783; 1786; 1798
        Sunday School library   1851
        U.S. (representative listing)   1731; 1733; 1737;
            1739; 1747; 1748; 1753; 1754; 1758; 1793; 1794;
            1796; 1827
        see also   Athenaeum; Colonial library; Mechanics'
            library; Mercantile library
Society library   see   Colonial library: Scholarly society;
            Social Library Movement
Special Library service   1909; 1910; 1915; 1941; 1948;
            1956
        Business   1904; 1913
        Film   1929; 1936; 1942; 1943; 1954; 1958
        see also   Photo-reproduction
        Hospital   1811; 1944
        Industrial   1867
        Law   1817; 1832; 1906; 1908
        Medical   1763; 1816; 1898; 1911; 1942; 1949
            Federal   1836; 1879; 1880; 1922; 1952; 1956
        Music   1882; 1897; 1931; 1934; 1951; 1954
        see also   Phono-reproduction
        Picture   1891; 1904
        see also   Illustrations (bk.)
        Technological   1830; 1889; 1913
        Theatre   1903; 1937; 1940

Special Library service cont.
     Theological 1791; 1947; 1953
     see also Federal library; Research library
Stacks see Shelving
Staff see Librarian
Standards
     Bibliography 1940
     College library 1959
     Education 1925; 1951
     Film 1936
     Medical library 1942
     Prison library 1944
     Public library . . .1921; 1933; 1943; 1948; 1956
     School library 1920; 1925
State aid see Aid (funds)
State libraries see National libraries
State library commission see Extension service
State library service (U.S.) 1818; 1889; 1956
Statutory copy see Deposit rights
Stereotype see Printing: Type-plates
Storage 1931 see also Depository library
Storage, Compact see Shelving
Storytelling programs see Public Library Movement
Student society library see Social Library Movement
Subject-headings lists
     ALA 1895
     LC 1909
     Sears 1923
     Special subject 1916; 1925; 1938; 1944
Subscription book 1617
Subscription library see Social Library Movement
Sunday School library see Social Library Movement
Surveys
     Adult education 1926; 1952
     Deterioration 1931
     Public library 1876; 1926; 1949
     Recruiting programs 1951
     Reference service 1956
     Television use 1955
Sutra see Book: Form & Make-up
Table of contents see Book: Form & Make-up
Talking-book see Non-book material
Taxes see Aid (funds)

Technical processes   see   Automation
Technological library   see   Special Library service
Telefacsim   see   Transcribing tool
Telegraph   1876; 1950
Television   1949; 1951; 1952; 1954; 1955
Terminology   see   Cooperative ventures
Theatre library   see   Special Library service
Theological library   see   Special Library service
3-plus-1 program   see   Education
Tiers   see   Shelving
Title-label   see   Book: Form & Make-up
Title page   see   Book: Form & Make-up
Trade catalog   see   Bibliography
Transcribing medium
     Alphabet   1st cent.
     Script   1st cent.; 400; 600
Transcribing surfaces
     Disc 1897
     Film 1928
     Paper . . . . 1st cent.;   105
     Papyrus . . . . 1st cent.
     Parchment . . . . 1st cent.
Transcribing tool
     Pen   1780
     Phono-record   see   Phono-reproduction
     Photograph   see   Photo-reproduction
     Punched card   see   Automation
     Telefacsim   1951
     Typewriter   1714; 1877; 1903
Translation service
     Checklist   1932; 1959
     Conference   1952
     Machine   1946; 1954; 1955
      Auto-digital   1947
      Dictionary   1948
Traveling library   1810; 1817; 1889; 1893; 1905
Trustees   see   Public Library Movement
Type foundry   see   Printing
Typewriter   see   Transcribing tool
Uncials   see   Transcribing medium: Script
Undergraduate library   1949
Union catalog service   1250; 1410; 1914; 1932
     NUC   1927; 1956; 1958

235

Union catalog service cont.
      U.S. (representative listing) 1914; 1921; 1932;
          1934; 1935; 1936; 1937; 1938; 1939; 1940
Union list service 1876; 1892; 1900; 1927
      Checklist 1899
      New Serials Titles 1951
      Union List of Microfilms 1941
      Union List of Serials 1927
Unions (labor) 1917; 1938
University press service 1478; 1521; 1869; 1878; 1944
Vertical file see Filing equipment
Voter registration see Public relations
Wartime services 1917; 1945
      see also Federal library: OWI
Watermarks see Paper
Weeding 1941; 1958
Woodcuts see Illustration (bk.): Engraving
Wood-engraving see Illustration (bk.): Engraving
Xerography see Printing
Xylography see Printing: Block-printing
YMCA library see Adult education
Yearbook see Reference tools
Young adults see Public Library Movement

Name Index

245

252